D0718715

NLP

made easy

Carol Harris is an independent consultant and trainer. Her practice, Management Magic, runs NLP-based courses in many areas of personal and business development, including personal effectiveness, presentation and facilitation skills, teambuilding, business writing, action learning and customer care.

Carol is a sociology graduate, a Fellow of the Institute of Personnel and Development and a Fellow (and council member) of the Institute of Management Consultancy. She is a Master Practitioner of NLP and was, for four years, Chair of the UK Association for Neuro-Linguistic Programming; she is also editor of the Association's quarterly magazine *Rapport*.

She is the author of *Networking for Success, Consult Yourself, Super Slimming* and *How to Produce Successful Magazines and Newsletters*, and has produced the *Success in Mind* series of audiotapes on personal effectiveness, which include the titles *Super Self, Handling Social Situations, Active Job Seeking, Creating a Good Impression* and *Super Slimming*. She is the publisher and editor of *Effective Consulting* magazine and has also written numerous articles for magazines and journals in the UK.

Carol Harris

NLP

made easy

An easy-to-follow
introduction to NLP

Element
An Imprint of HarperCollins*Publishers*
77–85 Fulham Palace Road
Hammersmith, London W6 8JB

The website address is:
www.thorsonselement.com

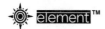

and *Element*
are trademarks of HarperCollins*Publishers* Limited

First published as *The Elements of NLP* by Element Books 1998
This edition published by Element 2003

10 9 8 7 6 5 4 3 2

© Carol Harris 1998, 2003

Some of the information on the history of NLP in the UK in
Chapter 2 was taken from various issues of *Rapport* magazine

Carol Harris asserts the moral right to
be identified as the author of this work

A catalogue record of this book
is available from the British Library

ISBN 0 00 715546 8

Printed and bound in Great Britain by
Martins The Printers Ltd, Berwick upon Tweed

All rights reserved. No part of this publication may be
reproduced, stored in a retrieval system, or transmitted,
in any form or by any means, electronic, mechanical,
photocopying, recording or otherwise, without the prior
written permission of the publishers.

Contents

Acknowledgements

This book is dedicated to David Gordon. On the final Practitioner course run by UKTC, David suggested that participants take on the role of 'experiential explorers', part of our brief being to think of what could possibly prevent us from continuing our interest and activity in NLP. My response was to say that what could put me off would be if I were unable to find new ways in which to explore the subject. I think it is fair to say that I have found new things to do with NLP ever since.

I would also like to thank the following people, whose assistance in producing this book has been invaluable: Paul Harris, for much of the research and support, Martin Roberts, for being a mine of information on NLP's chequered history, and Katrina Patterson, for her ongoing encouragement and assistance.

My thanks also go to my two NLP 'role models': Roy Johnson, who ran the very first NLP course I ever attended, and Douglas Pride, whose unique blend of humour, concern and entertainment is a real inspiration.

Note: Throughout this book I have credited sources wherever possible; if anyone has been left out this was entirely unintentional and any additional sources received will be noted for future editions.

Preface

My first encounter with NLP was reading the book which many other people had also acquired as their primer – *Frogs into Princes*. This book was both fascinating and confusing; it left many questions unanswered, as it was as a transcript of training rather than a stand-alone publication. However, for me, it was the impetus to further study and led to my professional life having a major focus on NLP.

If this book adds to the store of available knowledge on the subject of NLP, I hope it does so utilizing two concepts which have been important to me personally: structure and simplicity. I have aimed to make the book as straightforward as is possible; I have also aimed to use a structure which is easy to follow and where specific items can be pursued without having to wade through irrelevancies and jargon.

I would like to suggest a key in reading this book – and that is curiosity. Curiosity has long been a cornerstone of NLP. Attitudes of curiosity and exploration have led to the major developments which established NLP as a field in its own right and it is those same attitudes which continue to inform its progress. I would encourage you to approach each section of the book with these attitudes. Once you have read the book, it would be excellent if you could take the attitudes of curiosity and exploration forward into your life, extending your own personal search for knowledge, experience and creativity.

Finding your Way around this Book

Welcome to *NLP Made Easy*. There are many books on NLP, but what I have aimed at here is to provide a structured guide to the various elements of the topic. For the first time, there is a history of NLP in the UK; most published material has been based on the early origins of NLP in the United States, but it has a sound base in the UK, which deserves to be recorded. For this part of the book I am indebted to the writers who have submitted articles to *Rapport* (the magazine of the Association for Neuro-Linguistic Programming, of which I am the editor), giving their thoughts on the early days of NLP in the UK. I have also aimed to give a rather more detailed explanation of some of the NLP terms than is generally found in book glossaries. NLP can be very jargon-filled, which is perhaps understandable, given its history, but it can easily be practised without the use of complex terminology. However, given that that terminology is part of the inheritance of NLP, in the last section of the book I have provided some simple examples which I hope flesh out the basic terms in an understandable way.

The book is in three main parts:

★ Section One is about the origins and development of NLP and contains information on its history, notable people involved in its early development, and models, frameworks and techniques associated with it.

★ Section Two is about how you can apply NLP in your own life. This section includes three broad areas: personal growth, social relationships and business situations.

★ The appendices outline practical steps you can take if you wish to find out more about NLP, make use of the services of NLP-trained practitioners or pursue professional training in NLP yourself.

Each section has a brief introduction, outlining what is included and giving an overview of the topics covered. A more detailed explanation then follows.

The book can be read in a variety of ways, as each part has been designed to stand alone as well as to integrate with the rest of the book. You can choose to read it from start to finish, or you can select those sections which interest you most. If you prefer, you can look at the applications chapters first and then go back to read about the origins. A few topics are mentioned in more than one part of the book; this is intended to make the various sections as self-contained as possible.

NLP is very grounded in experience and I recommend that you take the time to do some of the exercises and activities. This will make the subject more real for you and give you a feel for how NLP actually works in practice. You might find it helpful to work through some of the exercises with another person and might also like to create a personal action plan, which will help you bring what you learn into everyday use.

I hope you enjoy finding out about this fascinating subject which has made a tremendous impact on so many people's lives.

Section One

This part of the book is about the history and development of NLP. Chapter 1 begins with some definitions of NLP and then goes on to put NLP in the broader context of developmental techniques. Chapter 2 covers the history of NLP and the contribution made by some of the notable figures in the NLP world. Chapter 3 introduces some of the best-known NLP frameworks, models and techniques.

Because NLP is continuously growing and developing, this section gives only a snapshot taken at the present time; five or ten years from now there will, no doubt, be further changes and innovations. If you are seriously interested in NLP, it is worth keeping up with its development and the appendices give you some ideas on how you can do that.

Chapter 1

What is Neuro-Linguistic Programming?

This chapter introduces you to Neuro-Linguistic Programming (NLP) and gives an outline of where it originated, what it covers and how it works, together with some of its links with other disciplines. It also considers popular misconceptions about NLP and gives a brief guide to ongoing developments in the field.

You probably already 'do' NLP and are likely to know a good deal about some of its approaches. This is because NLP has its roots in real-life behaviour, rather than in theory and research. NLP is about how people become successful at things; how they achieve what they aim for and enhance their lives. NLP encompasses a wide variety of processes and techniques, and has an overriding emphasis and approach – that of curiosity, exploration and action. NLP can offer you many things, but it helps if you are willing to be adventurous, open to change and fascinated by life and all that it brings.

NLP's main aim is to help people get better at what they do. Its focus on performance has a number of principles, some of which are as follows:

★ Excellence in performance can be modelled (analysed) and trans-
ferred from one person to another.
★ High performance requires both the development of skills and
development of corresponding mental and physical states.
★ Mental and physical states can be broken down into small measurable elements and modified to achieve desired results.

What distinguishes NLP from many other disciplines is its focus on
modelling (*see Chapter 3*). Briefly, modelling is the elicitation of sets
of patterns; in NLP, patterns which demonstrate how people achieve
excellence in performance. These patterns can be copied by others in
order to replicate the achievements of high performers. Characteristic
features of NLP are its specific techniques for analysing the components
of performance, especially how the mind processes information and
installs strategies for achievement. It can do this across all areas of personal and professional performance, including motivation, learning,
maintaining good health, sports performance, communication, negotiating, public speaking, teambuilding and change management.

NLP's processes of modelling are distinct from NLP's applications (for
example techniques for enhancing sales, negotiating, teaching and so
forth). Many people believe that NLP *is* its techniques, but the techniques are simply a minor part of a field of study which is, in essence, a
holistic and systemic approach to understanding personal and organizational effectiveness.

Richard Bandler, a co-founder of NLP, has been quoted as saying that,
to master NLP, it is necessary to 'let it completely permeate your thinking and feeling' and that it involves 'a ferocious spirit of "going for it" –
characteristics of "excitement", "curiosity", "high level state management of your own moods", "passion" and "commitment"' (Michael L.
Hall, *The Spirit of NLP*, The Anglo-American Book Co Ltd, 1996). John
Grinder, another co-founder of NLP, says that people wanting to train or

represent NLP in any way 'need to possess qualities of personal congruity, sparkling intelligence, a deep bottomless curiosity, a driving desire to discover new patterning, a phobic class response to repeating themselves, a continuous scanning for evidence that they are mistaken in every aspect of their personal and professional beliefs, solid personal ethics, physical fitness, actual real world experience in any field in which they intend to present NLP and an excellent sense of humour' (Internet interview – Inspirative 1996).

NLP provides ways of helping anyone become more competent at what they do, more in control of their thoughts, feelings and actions, more positive in their approach to life and better able to achieve results. If people do not have, within themselves, the knowledge or resources to achieve what they want, NLP makes it possible for them to adapt other people's skills and ways of thinking and incorporate them within their own lives in order to be more successful. NLP is, as one definition has succinctly put it, 'the Art and Science of Excellence'.

Definitions

Because of its nature, different people perceive different things in NLP and gain different things from it; definitions of NLP, therefore, are numerous and varied. As well as the one given above, they have included the following:

★ 'an attitude which is an insatiable curiosity about human beings with a methodology that leaves behind it a trail of techniques' (Richard Bandler)
★ 'an owner's guide to the mind'
★ 'the study of subjective experience'

★ 'the study of the structure of subjectivity' (Dilts, Bandler, Grinder, DeLozier, *Neuro-Linguistic Programming: Volume 1*)
★ 'software for the brain'
★ 'a new Science of Achievement'
★ 'the study of human excellence'
★ 'the ability to be your best more often'
★ 'the science that teaches how to use the neurological and linguistic resources in order to follow the program of self preservation, health and happiness in union with other people and nature' (Luis Jorge Gonzales)
★ 'a manual for the structured use of creativity' (Roz Carroll)
★ 'how to think positively so you can enhance your performance'
★ 'an adventure in experience'

As most of these definitions focus on personal improvement, one way of thinking of NLP is to consider it as providing a way of helping people move from situations which could be improved to situations which are better. Whereas other disciplines, such as psychology, give insights into human behaviour and motivation, NLP actually provides practical ways of improving performance. So it incorporates a technology for bringing about change in people, a set of approaches and tools which combine to offer ideas and skills for enhancing how people do things.

This can be summed up by saying that NLP helps people identify their present states (how they think and feel, what they do and the results they achieve), consider their desired states (what they would really like instead) and learn how to move from one to the other. It is not prescriptive about what the desired states should be, leaving that to the individual. For example, two people might both wish to become better at responding to other people's criticism. The first person might become upset when criticized (their 'present state') and wish to 'be able to accept criticism in a positive way', while the second person might become defensive when criticized and wish to 'be able to be receptive and use the criticism to bring about personal change'. Both people could be helped to achieve their aims using NLP techniques, but NLP does not tell them that one aim is 'correct' or 'more desirable' than another (although it can help them consider the advantages and disadvantages of each).

To achieve the transition from present state to desired state, there are three elements which NLP considers: *you* (your own situation and disposition); *others* (those with whom you are dealing) and *flexibility* (the possibility of varying what you do in order to be effective).

Origins

We will be covering the history of NLP in the next chapter; the following is just a very brief outline to put the rest of this chapter into context.

NLP in its present form originated in the early 1970s in the USA, although much of it was based on concepts and approaches that were considerably older. The contribution of the founders to NLP as a discrete field of study was twofold: first, the codification, enlargement and extension of previously existing concepts into a practically useful developmental tool; and second, the promotion of 'modelling' (*see Chapter 3*) to replicate excellence in performance.

NLP stands for Neuro-Linguistic Programming, a title given to it by two of its major founders, Richard Bandler and John Grinder, although the term 'neuro-linguistic' had been coined by Alfred Korzybski much earlier and appeared in print in his book *Science and Sanity* in 1933. *Neuro* relates to the mind and how it works; *linguistic* relates to the ways in which people express or communicate their experience of the world; *programming* relates to the fact that people behave according to personal 'programmes' which govern their ways of being in the world. So NLP encompasses the ways in which people think and act in their everyday lives.

California in the 1970s was a hotbed of ideas and activities. Richard Bandler and John Grinder (*see Chapter 2*) began exploring how really effective people achieved their results. They turned their attention to a number of individuals, each of whom excelled in their own field, the three best-known of whom were Milton Erickson, Virginia Satir and Fritz Perls (*see Chapter 2*).

In studying these people who excelled in their professions, Bandler and Grinder were curious to explore what was 'the difference that made the difference' – in other words what, specifically, led these people to excel. They found that each of their subjects exhibited specific personal patterns of behaviour and thinking, and it is these patterns, with their component elements, which form much of the basis for NLP.

So what are the elements involved in people's patterns? Although not originally put into a specific unified model, certain discrete elements are involved; in particular thoughts, feelings and behaviour – in other words, how people *think*, how they *feel* and what they *do*. These three elements are the foundation of performance. Other elements can be added, in particular *objectives, beliefs/values/attitudes* and *spirituality*. (In taking these elements as key, I have drawn upon the work of David Gordon, Graham Dawes and Robert Dilts, and the next part of this chapter is based especially on the Experiential Dynamics model of Gordon and Dawes; *see Chapter 3*.)

What Bandler, Grinder and their colleagues noticed was that the people they studied had ways (or patterns) of thinking, feeling and behaving which made them effective. The people were not always aware of these patterns, but they could be noticed by keen outside observers. The conclusions reached were that once you can observe and describe such patterns, they can be copied by others. This meant that other people could learn to follow the same patterns in order to achieve similar results.

Now there is nothing startlingly new in this process; it is how much learning takes place. For example, to learn how to tie a shoelace a child has to copy (model) how someone else does it. What makes NLP particularly effective is its ability to break performance down into very small elements and to take account of 'internal' processes such as thoughts and feelings, as well as 'external' behaviour, when helping others to learn and develop.

Utilizing and Working with the Patterns

If we take each element of a pattern in turn – objectives, behaviour, thoughts, feelings and beliefs – we can see how NLP enables people to explore and enhance their performance. Later I will be returning to some of these aspects and showing how you can use them personally in your own development.

Objectives
There are already well-established approaches to objective setting, for example the SMART approach (*see Chapter 6*). NLP goes beyond these, and helps define objectives in a way which makes it much more likely that they will be achieved. To do this, NLP uses what it calls Well Formed Outcomes, or WFOs. The WFO model for setting effective objectives is covered in detail in Chapter 6 and is the foundation for effective NLP work; by ensuring that objectives are well defined, progress and change are facilitated.

Behaviour

Behaviour is the only thing which is observable by others; they cannot see into your mind or know how you are feeling unless you either tell them or show them – and both of these processes (telling and showing) are behaviour. So NLP works with all aspects of behaviour, helping people to observe and respond to behaviour in useful and appropriate ways.

Some specific ways in which NLP works with behaviour are the following:

Helping people to learn skills

This often involves 'role modelling' someone with excellent skills in a particular field and learning how to transfer these skills to another person. Examples of this could include playing a musical instrument (finding out which techniques are used by professional musicians and emulating them) or taking part in sports (selecting top performers in different sporting fields – for example golf, athletics, tennis – and breaking down their performance into component parts in order to replicate it).

Creating and maintaining rapport and influence

NLP has specific ways of enhancing rapport and influence, notably the concept of 'matching' (or copying) other people in order to make them feel at ease. The idea is that most people feel comfortable with others who are similar to themselves, so by making yourself a little more like another person you can enhance their feelings of comfort and acceptance (*see also Chapter 5*).

Using language to communicate and influence

There are a number of aspects here, including the following:

★ recognizing people's personality and motivational patterns through their language patterns

★ recognizing which senses people favour or rely on, through listening to the actual words they use

★ being able to use either precise or imprecise language where appropriate to achieve particular results

★ using indirect language for persuasiveness and influence

★ respecting the actual words and phrases used by individuals, as those words represent their experience of reality

Language will be covered in more detail in Chapters 4–6.

Thoughts

The elements of thought involve seeing (visualizing), hearing (imagining sounds or having 'internal conversations' or dialogue in one's head), experiencing sensations (emotional or tactile), sensing smells or sensing tastes. In each of these areas, NLP enables people to notice their thoughts and then, if needed, to modify them and thereby their experience.

For example, you might ask someone to think about a flower. First they can imagine how the flower looks (its colour and shape), then imagine how it smells (its scent), then imagine how it feels (its form and texture), then imagine how it sounds (perhaps its leaves rustling in a breeze), then imagine how it tastes (some flowers are edible!) So far, the experience has been imitating reality – you have asked the person to imagine a real flower, as it is usually perceived. Now for the interesting part: you can ask the person to manipulate their mental experience to create something entirely new. So, for example, you might ask the person to imagine the flower a different colour, a different size, with a different smell, making an unusual sound, and so forth. The ability of the mind to make these changes is a foundation for learning and innovation, and if you have never experimented in such a manner, you may be amazed at the changes in experience which such shifts can bring about.

Because of its ability to manipulate the senses, NLP can help people create more (or less) pleasant experiences for themselves. And in case you are wondering why they should want to create a less pleasant experience, think of how to teach someone to avoid putting their hand in a hot fire, or how to make sure they don't drive after they have been drinking.

Feelings

NLP was largely founded on the activities of therapists and it has continued to emphasize the importance of a balanced emotional state in achieving effective performance. It has techniques for managing emotions, many of them involving the sensory shifts referred to in the previous section. Emotional responses are often brought about by thoughts and are certainly closely linked to them, so by changing thought patterns it is often easy to change emotional responses.

Another way in which NLP engages the emotions is through its association with behaviour. Because there is a close link between body and mind, by making changes in the body, changes in the mind – and thereby the emotions – often follow. An example of this is posture. Most people have habitual postures associated with different emotional states, for example being more upright when energetic and taking up less space when apprehensive. By changing posture it is possible to change the thoughts and feelings which follow. So, to get someone to feel more energetic, it is possible to identify their personal posture for energy and then help them re-create it; once they have done so, they are more likely to feel energetic. The same goes for states such as calmness, relaxation, motivation, enthusiasm and so forth – certain postures are more likely to produce each of these states in a given person.

Beliefs

One of NLP's strengths is its ability to influence change at deep levels. Although change can be brought about by teaching people new skills, it is beliefs, values and assumptions which are the foundation of each individual.

Much of NLP is about changes in beliefs, values and attitudes, sometimes direct and sometimes indirect. For example, a direct belief change could be brought about by confronting a person with an example which contradicts their previous experience; maybe showing them a yellow tomato if they believed tomatoes were always red or encouraging a person from a minority group to apply for (and get) a senior job which they had believed was beyond their reach. An indirect belief change could be brought about through exposing a person to different learning situations which, cumulatively, resulted in them changing their beliefs, for example giving a person who believed they were poor at public speaking the opportunity to practise until they were convinced they could do it. Equally, assumptions may be changed when a person gains a different perspective on a situation, for example a person who thinks a neighbour is being indifferent to them, but then finds out the person is hard of hearing and has not been able to hear what is being said.

The interesting thing about the way in which NLP works to effect such changes is that it can help people experience changes in their mind, rather than having to put them in 'real-life' situations to face real (or imagined) obstacles. It has been found that people have actual mental 'locations' for beliefs and that by helping a person to locate and utilize these locations, it is possible to influence the strength of their beliefs.

Spirituality

NLP also offers ways of exploring what is 'beyond' everyday experience. Spirituality is a rather different concept from the other elements I have been discussing, ie behaviour, thoughts, feelings and beliefs. These elements are easier to communicate, as people are likely to have more of a shared understanding of them. For example, in discussing behaviour, it is relatively easy to discuss whether a shop assistant has been helpful or uninterested, or whether a student is listening or distracted; these things are relatively easy to observe and construe. With spirituality, however, each person's experience is both 'internal' and personal and the vocabulary with which to discuss it is frequently more limited.

For example, two people may visit an area of countryside where they can enjoy seeing the landscape, hearing the sounds of animals, feeling the sunshine and being aware of the scents in the air. One person may simply experience this as a pleasant day out; for the other person the outing may provide an awareness of something beyond the immediate experience, perhaps a sense of fulfilment, of integration, or of a power or quality which permeates the senses. While being acutely conscious of this personal experience, it may be difficult for the second person to explain in everyday language what their awareness actually is.

Despite these limitations, many people working with NLP are helping others to develop their spiritual sense and awareness.

Features of NLP

NLP has some specific features which mark it out; other disciplines may have one or more of these, but the combination of all makes NLP distinctive. What are these features?

It takes a holistic approach
NLP takes the view that all parts of a person are interrelated and that changes in one part impinge or reflect on all the others. This

approach ensures that the overall consequences of any change process is considered.

It works with micro-details

In contrast to being holistic, NLP is also often concerned with minute detail. An example of this is the way in which it works with specific elements of thought processes, such as how people visualize and how they use 'internal dialogue'. NLP enables people to analyse such processes in a way that helps them be more effective. Working with detail often helps understanding and assimilation and makes it possible to work on one element at a time, rather than being swamped by multiple activities.

It is based on competency and role modelling

NLP is very much to do with individual skills and abilities. In this respect it ties in well with current approaches to training and development. The foundation of NLP is 'modelling' (*see Chapter 3*), especially 'role modelling' effective people, finding out precisely which elements of their performance are contributing to their success, and then helping others to perform in a similar manner.

It focuses on mental processing

Although a good deal of NLP is about behaviour, much of it is about how people's thoughts influence their performance. NLP offers ways of modifying mental patterns (or strategies) and helping people make changes in these to help enhance their lives.

It utilizes specific language patterns

Utilization of language patterns provides powerful techniques for interacting with others and bringing about change. NLP has a wide range of language processes and patterns that can be applied in a variety of contexts.

It works with both the conscious and the unconscious mind

The terms 'conscious' and 'unconscious' have been used in various parts of this book. The state of consciousness is generally recognizable as an awareness of oneself or elements in one's environment (or beyond).

The term 'unconscious' is commonly applied to states such as sleep, anaesthesia or fainting, but can also be used to describe mental processes that are 'out of awareness'. These 'out-of-awareness' processes can include a wide range of things; for example having a mannerism of which one is not consciously aware, becoming familiar with a language simply by being exposed to hearing it rather than consciously taking time to learn the words or grammar, or responding to something in an automatic way without being aware of why that is happening (for example considering a person attractive because the pupils of their eyes are dilated, but not being aware that that fact is influencing your reaction).

Although there are differing views on how, or whether, unconscious processes actually exist (they could simply be pre-programmed behaviour rather than evidence of an 'unconscious' part of the mind), there is a general acceptance that the unconscious mind does exist and has a powerful influence on our attitudes and behaviour. This influence may be either positive or negative, resulting in behaviour which either achieves beneficial results or hinders them. The recognition of the influence of the unconscious mind informs much of NLP's work, so that, although it is possible to use NLP to work solely at a conscious level, for example to break down a skill into concrete parts in order to teach it, it is probably most effective when it integrates conscious/unconscious processing. For example, when teaching a skill to people who believe that they will find it hard to learn, it is possible to manage the process of teaching so that it incorporates elements which reach the unconscious mind and are directly absorbed by the learner at a deep level.

A note of caution should be added here. Because some techniques appear to work directly at an unconscious level, bypassing conscious awareness, they could be open to misuse or could inadvertently cause undesirable results. Such techniques should therefore only be used after sufficient training and with the safeguards of respect and concern for the person who is 'on the receiving end'. For this reason, certain techniques have only been described in outline in this book, so that they will not be practised without sufficient guidance and skill.

It is rapid in its processes and results

A major feature of NLP is the speed with which it can produce results. Many NLP techniques are extremely rapid in their application (the most famous probably being the 'fast phobia cure', which can successfully be carried out in a matter of minutes). Because of the speed of such processes, many people do not believe they can really work and are therefore sceptical about NLP as a whole. Current thinking, however, is that the brain works (and learns) speedily and therefore change can be brought about rapidly. This is in contradiction to many traditional approaches, especially that of psychoanalysis, which maintain that lengthy courses of treatment – often running into years – and taking people back into the past, instead of having the future focus that is characteristic of NLP, are necessary to bring about insight and change.

It is neutral as an approach

NLP as an approach is neutral. It is a tool, not a prescription. How NLP is used depends entirely on the practitioner and the user/client. There are as many ways of using NLP as there are people working with it.

It is respectful in how it treats people

An interesting thing about NLP is that one of its principles involves respect for others; its importance is instilled from the early stages in training. Because of this, attention is paid to what is termed 'ecology', which in NLP means the circumstances surrounding any particular intervention. To be ecological means considering the broader context of an intervention, paying attention to the needs and wishes of the person/s with whom you are working, taking into account their point of view as well as your own beliefs about what is desirable. This emphasis on ethics makes NLP stand out from many other disciplines.

Presuppositions

Another feature of NLP is its 'presuppositions'. These are statements which are not necessarily held to be 'true', but used as *assumptions* which influence strongly the behaviour and responses of those using NLP. Here are some of NLP's commonest presuppositions:

Experience has structure
There are patterns to how we think about/organize our experience, and if we change these patterns, our experience changes with it.

A map is not the territory
People's perceptions are subjective; what you perceive is selective, not a complete, or necessarily true, account of reality. So, for example, a colour-blind person would not perceive certain distinctions in colour, but this does not mean they do not exist. Similarly, a person might construe another's behaviour as malevolent, but this might not be the case. We see and respond according to our own selectively filtered 'maps of the world' and helping people understand theirs, and acknowledge those of others, is a feature of NLP.

The mind and body are one system

What we do with our minds and our bodies is interlinked. For example, sitting in a particular posture can lead us to feel a particular emotion; similarly, a positive thought will have an effect on our physiology. There is currently much emphasis on the interrelation of mind and body on health (for example the use of visualization in helping fight cancer) and the field of PNI (psychoneuroimmunology) is demonstrating such links on an ongoing basis.

People work perfectly

Instead of thinking of people as faulty because they do not do what seems to be appropriate, conventional or effective, it is useful to think of them as being extremely effective at getting particular results, even though these results may not be the 'best' in the circumstances. So, for example, someone who has a phobia, say of spiders, is excellent at maintaining a frightened response; this may be inappropriate for house spiders, but could be a real help in keeping away from poisonous spiders in a tropical country.

If something is possible for one person it is possible for everybody

This does not mean that everyone can be an Olympic athlete, brain surgeon or artist; it simply means that if something *can* be done by one person, then *potentially* everyone could do it, given suitable resources. This presupposition is helpful in encouraging people to extend their performance beyond what they might previously have believed possible.

Everyone has all the resources they need

People have within themselves a vast reservoir of 'internal' abilities and attributes; achievement is generally more about what you bring to a situation than external elements.

There is no failure, only feedback

If you do not achieve what you set out to, this can be taken as useful information to help you in your future endeavours, rather than as evidence that you are incapable of achieving what you desire.

If what you are doing isn't working, do something else

Flexibility is a key to effectiveness; if you vary what you do until you get a result, you are more likely to be effective than if you continue to carry out behaviour which is not getting you to where you want to be.

You do the best you can at the time

Although, with hindsight, many things could be done differently, we can only make the best choice at the time. This does not mean that we always make the 'right' decision; simply that decisions are based on 'best guesses' at the time. ('New code' NLP might take a different view of this and help us listen more to our 'body signals', but more of that in Chapter 3.)

Every behaviour has a positive intent

Even the most negative-seeming behaviour is done for a purpose. This is a useful assumption to make when dealing with others, as it enables you to consider why they behave as they do, to explore their real needs and, possibly, to find alternative ways of meeting them.

The meaning of the communication is the response you get

It is the perception of the receiver that determines the effectiveness of interaction, not the intention of the initiator.

Almost all the presuppositions have been debated at length, for example the proposal that all behaviour has a positive intent, or the fact that what is possible for one person is potentially possible for all. However, the point of the presuppositions is to enable people to extend themselves and to perceive opportunities and benefits in situations. By acting as if the presuppositions were true, it is amazing what can be achieved.

Associations

Where did NLP come from? Many of the ideas used in NLP originated in much earlier times. Certainly many of the concepts were known about decades ago and some were mentioned, although in very different terminology, centuries ago. There are, however, a number of specific connections between NLP and other established disciplines, in particular the following:

★ **Applied psychology:** It is easy to think of NLP as a branch of applied psychology. To label it in this way is really to diminish its impact, as it goes beyond the bounds of traditional psychology, but it is probably a good initial way of considering it. One explanation of how NLP goes beyond conventional psychology is as follows: 'While traditional clinical psychology is primarily concerned with describing difficulties, categorizing them, and searching for historical causes, NLP is interested in *how* our thoughts, actions, and feelings work together right now to produce our experience.' (Faulkner) There is also a link with psychometric testing (and some Jungian 'traits') in the use of one of the NLP language patterns called Meta-Programmes (*see Chapter 5*).

★ **Gestalt psychology/psychotherapy:** One of the early role models for NLP was Fritz Perls, the reputed father of Gestalt psychotherapy. Gestalt relates to the linkages between elements, so that an entity can be understood through the interrelationships of its parts; the parts alone do not necessarily make sense. (One area of NLP deals with 'parts' and that will be covered in more detail in Chapter 3.)

★ **Ericksonian hypnosis:** Another early role model was Milton Erickson and his influence on NLP has been enormous. Unlike classical hypnosis, the Ericksonian approach is seemingly low key and unobtrusive. Much use is made of indirect language, suggestion and utilization of the patient/client/subject's own patterns of speaking, breathing and moving in order to bring about change. Erickson himself was expert at adapting his approach to the specific needs of the individual with whom he was working and this way of working has informed many of NLP's later practitioners (although the indirect approach is closely linked with Erickson, he was substantially influenced by classical hypnosis and did use a lot of direct techniques himself).

★ **Systems thinking/cybernetics:** Much of NLP utilizes systems thinking. Work by Ashby, Beer and others has had a major impact on how NLP has developed and been used and many of the NLP models presented in Chapter 3 explore the systemic nature of different areas of experience.

★ **Linguistics:** Much of NLP originated in the work of linguists, including Korzybski and Chomsky. Such people had laid down many of the principles which underlie NLP's language patterns. Some of the connections which have been made are with the ways in which language represents experience, especially in a metaphorical sense, and the ways in which language demonstrates people's underlying motivational and behavioural patterns.

In addition, some topics that are becoming associated with NLP are:

★ **Accelerated learning:** Accelerated learning puts much emphasis on the needs of the individual and the helpfulness of recognizing and utilizing individual patterns in order to enhance learning and development. The earliest writer on this topic was the Bulgarian Georgi Lozanov, working in the 1960s, and other famous names in the field are Ostrander, Schroeder and Jenson, who have written at length about how to improve trainer/trainee relationships. In particular, accelerated learning puts the onus on the trainer to ensure that the learner is in a resourceful state in which to learn, and this means that learning is not simply a one-way process of pushing information towards a recipient and hoping it will stick, but involves creating an atmosphere and an environment in which interaction and mutual respect can lead to individual growth.

★ **Bodywork:** NLP is increasingly being associated with the field of physical development as well as psychological enhancement. Some examples of current links are the Alexander Technique, Feldenkrais, kinesiology, tai chi, voicework/singing, and so forth. With all of these techniques, practitioners use a mixture of body movement and mental/emotional control to achieve results.

NLP constantly draws upon other disciplines and approaches to integrate appropriate parts of them with its own ways of working. Because of this, NLP is evolving all the time and, while it remains recognizable, is fluid and flexible.

Misconceptions

Having explained what NLP is, it is also important to mention what NLP is not. There are several popular misconceptions about NLP and the following questions are often asked by people new to NLP:

Isn't NLP just positive thinking?

Well, yes, in a way, but it goes far beyond simply having nice thoughts and actually gives people a way of knowing *what* to do in order to think positively. For example, some years ago a training video was produced on presentation skills. The video told viewers that it was important, when making a presentation, to *feel confident*. However, no advice was offered on how to do that! NLP makes it possible to offer such advice by being able to identify specific things that can be done to master thoughts and feelings as well as behaviour.

Isn't NLP manipulative?

Most things can be used in a manipulative way, although they themselves are simply neutral tools. For example a motor car can be driven in such a way that it becomes a hazard, or a person collecting money for an animal charity could take along a sorry-looking small furry animal to elicit feelings of sympathy in passers by. NLP as an approach, like the motor car or the small animal, is neutral; it does not impose rules for its use. So how you use NLP is as important as what you use it for; it is ultimately up to you to determine whether it is used ethically or not.

How can NLP be taken seriously if it claims to work so quickly?

The problem with this question is that it presupposes certain limitations. If you are used to things taking a long time, speed may be suspicious. For example, you could say it takes years of study to learn the differences between wild plants, but one encounter with a stinging nettle could well imprint its appearance, smell and feel indelibly on your mind! Because conventional psychological approaches have traditionally been time-consuming, it can be difficult to believe that work with NLP can be as fast as it is; the proof, however, is in the results, not in the hype.

Is it really a separate field of study?

This question often comes from people used to thinking about subjects in a very tightly defined way and it has been said that NLP draws on so many other disciplines that it is not a discrete field in itself. Although it has drawn upon many other disciplines, NLP does have unique elements of its own, some of which were covered at the beginning of this chapter in the section on 'Features of NLP'. It is probably the focus on the practical applications of mental processing which most distinguishes NLP from other disciplines. It also has established programmes of study, with recognized qualifications at different levels, making it a discipline which is unique and identifiable.

The Future of NLP

From the start, NLP has been evolving and developing. Its main founders are still active and developing new concepts and approaches, as are others newer to the field. For the future, we can anticipate further refinements, more applications and innovation and creativity in NLP's further development.

Chapter 2

The History of NLP

In the last chapter, some of the origins of NLP were discussed and some people associated with its development mentioned. This section takes a more in-depth look at these origins, both in the USA and the UK, and at some of the people who have been a great influence on the emergence and continuation of NLP, some by contributing new techniques and approaches and some by popularizing NLP to a wider audience.

NLP in the USA

NLP as a defined field of study originated in the USA in the early 1970s although, as mentioned in the last chapter, there were many influences on its development, going back decades (including likely links to US Air Force/CIA research on language, modelling, eye movements and so forth) or, in the case of some of the ideas themselves, centuries.

In the late 1950s, a group of people had come together in Palo Alto, California, in what became known as the Communication Research Project. Led by Gregory Bateson *(see below)* it studied communications, psychotherapy, brief therapy and animal behaviour. A further group was set up later at the Mental Research Institute (MRI), the best-known members of which were Paul Watzlawick and the late David Weakland. This group was generally referred to as the Palo Alto Group. The group looked at the approaches and techniques of current practitioners, including Perls, Satir, Erickson and Huxley, considering what they did and said that had an effect on others; in other words, their processes as well as the content of their communications and activities. The Palo Alto work led to further research at Stanford University and was a major influence on the early developers of NLP.

The focus of activity for NLP itself was, initially, the University at Santa Cruz, California, where the Dean had a vision of creating an environment where different disciplines, ideas and models could come together in a creative way. This whole area of California was a hotbed of ideas and development, including Santa Cruz, Palo Alto and Big Sur, where the famous Esalen Institute was to be formed. In this climate, a group of people at Santa Cruz became interested in personal enhancement, creativity and communications. The underpinning drive which lay behind most of the group's activities was that of curiosity. This period has been written about in many books on NLP, including *The Wild Days: NLP 1972–1981* by Terrence L. McClendon, which gives a highly personal account of the period.

NLP's best-known founders, Richard Bandler and John Grinder, became part of the wider group at Santa Cruz, working on aspects of development. Bandler studied a range of topics – initially physics and computing, then psychology, philosophy, maths and other subjects. He was also a talented musician. Becoming disillusioned with existing university courses, he explored ways of bringing about practical changes in the fields in which he was working. One of his particular interests was Gestalt psychology and he started to teach seminars in Gestalt Therapy.

Bandler formed a close association with John Grinder, who was Assistant Professor of Linguistics at Santa Cruz. Grinder had gained a

PhD in San Francisco, where his language studies included the theories of Noam Chomsky, the American linguist. He had been an interpreter in the US army and had engaged in covert operations. He was very experienced in working with language through 'modelling' *(see Chapter 3)*, and had learned several languages using this process.

As Bandler had exceptional skills in absorbing other people's behavioural patterns (in the early days he was referred to as a sponge, because of this ability to 'become' another person) and Grinder had great experience of modelling (and was sometimes referred to as a chameleon because of his ability to 'change his colours without changing himself'), they began working together, with Bandler showing Grinder what he did and Grinder helping him model it. Together they analysed the performance of many people, including some leading therapists – initially Fritz Perls and Virginia Satir, and later Milton Erickson. Although Virginia Satir and Milton Erickson were available face to face, Perls had already died and Bandler's analysis of how he worked came from studying videotapes of him. It has been reported that Bandler became so focused on Perls that after lengthy periods with the video machine, he would emerge looking and sounding just like Perls, with a German accent and a stoop, and smoking heavily.

Together with Bandler and Grinder, a group formed, working on the various elements which became the foundations of NLP. Each of the emerging techniques was explored and refined on an ongoing basis. As well as working on NLP, people were experimenting with hypnotic techniques and language, including deep trance states, positive and negative hallucination, time distortion and amnesia. Terrence McClendon, in *The Wild Days*, remarks on the association between NLP and hypnosis: 'You could say that the NLP techniques are the conscious mind's model of how the unconscious mind works in hypnosis.'

It is difficult to attribute the emergence of a particular NLP technique to a particular 'creator', as the efforts of the whole Santa Cruz group often interrelated in order to allow these forms to emerge. As work continued, the different elements of NLP gradually emerged and many of its original creators and developers are still making further refinements and extensions.

Personal associations were also formed during the period in California. In 1977 Bandler married Leslie Cameron and she became Leslie Cameron Bandler. They were married by Grinder, who was a preacher from the Universal Light Church. The marriage lasted only a year or so. Grinder himself later married Judith DeLozier, with whom he formed Grinder, DeLozier and Associates after parting company with Bandler in the 1980s. His marriage also came to an end some while later and he is now in partnership with Carmen Bostic St Clair.

While they were still working together, Bandler and Grinder set up the Society of Neuro-Linguistic Programming, originally as a partnership between Bandler's company Not Limited and Grinder's company Limited Unlimited. They also formed a publishing company called Meta Publications, which was responsible for many of the notable books in the field of NLP.

In 1977 the Division of Training and Research (DOTAR), a training, development and research operation, was set up in Santa Cruz by Richard Bandler, John Grinder, Judith DeLozier, Leslie Cameron, Maribeth Anderson, Robert Dilts and David Gordon. This was the first NLP training institute and Leslie Cameron was overall Director, David Gordon was Director of Training and Robert Dilts was Director of Research.

By late 1976, some of the people who had been attending Bandler and Grinder's workshops started to run their own. These people included Byron Lewis, Robert Dilts, Terrence McClendon and Steve Stevens (later Andreas). Also Leslie Cameron Bandler and Judith DeLozier began presenting workshops together.

As the field grew, so some of the original associations began to change and, in particular, the partnership between Richard Bandler and

John Grinder came to an end in the early 1980s. Their interests had begun to diverge and they also had different ideas about what the future held in store for NLP. Both, however, continued to be driving forces within NLP and continue to train and write to this day.

NLP was, from its inception, very much about practicalities and application, rather than theory. Questions such as 'How can this be used?' and 'How can this be taught?' were asked frequently. The legacy of the Santa Cruz group lies, at least in part, in the attitudes of curiosity and usefulness which informed its work. As NLP continues to develop, questions about application and transfer are still foremost in the minds of many working in the field.

NLP in the UK

While NLP began life in the USA, the United Kingdom became a focal point for much activity and innovation, with two main strands to its development, involving Eileen Watkins Seymour and Graham Dawes. Together with Gene Early, Ian Cunningham and David Gaster, they made contacts which led to the foundation of the UK Training Centre for Neuro-Linguistic Programming (UKTC).

In Eileen Watkins Seymour's account of how the field developed in Britain, she relates how in 1979 she was contacted by a fellow student on a humanistic psychology master's programme in London and agreed to host a meeting with Gene Early and others who were interested in the subject.

Around a dozen people gathered and from this original meeting a study group was formed, which met on a fortnightly basis. Some of the people involved at that time were Michael Mallows, Willie Monteiro, Graham Dawes, Vivienne Gill, John Watson and Frank Kevlin, who later became Chair of the UK Association for Neuro-Linguistic Programming.

By the following year, members of the group became interested in starting some NLP training and Eileen, Gene Early, Graham Dawes, David Gaster and Ian Cunningham initiated the first Diploma programme in the UK, at the London Business School, and the UK Training Centre (UKTC) was born. The Diploma programme lasted eight months, with a focus on quality in both the training and the elements surrounding it. At the time it was the only full-scale NLP training anywhere outside North America.

The aim of the UKTC was to grow people, not to make money, and the whole ethos of the organization reflected this. Sessions ran from Friday evening through the entire weekend. The first group consisted of 30 people, many of them therapists, and as well as the weekend training, everyone went to a weekly study group. Early trainers on the programme included Gene Early, Barbara Witney, David Gaster, David Gordon and Robert Dilts. Charlotte Bretto and Dave Dobson were also early trainers. Later, master's programmes were offered, as well as speciality workshops given by visiting trainers from overseas.

By 1987, David Gaster had moved on and Gene Early and Graham Dawes felt it time to hand over the reins. Dudley and Regan Masters, trainers who had graduated from the UKTC, were given the Centre. Eileen was still keen to continue, but decided to 'let go of [her] baby'. The UKTC only lasted for two further years and was then wound up. Dudley and Regan Masters have not been seen on the NLP scene since and word has it that they became born-again Christians. David Gaster, sadly, died a few years ago. Eileen, in conjunction with Clive Digby-Jones (now her husband), founded and still runs the Ravenscroft Centre in London. Graham Dawes continues his activities in NLP, as does Gene Early. Both are respected figures in their communities.

Several early graduates of the UKTC subsequently set up their own training centres in the UK. Some of the earliest ones were PACE, John Seymour Associates, NLP Training Program, Pace Personal Development and Sensory Systems, as well as associated bodies such as British Hypnosis Research and the Proudfoot School of Hypnosis.

Currently there are over 50 UK training organizations and although it is increasingly difficult to pinpoint individuals or individual organizations as 'leading edge', there are many innovative steps being taken which contribute to the development, and professionalism, of NLP in the UK.

In addition to the training organizations, numerous networking and practice groups have sprung up throughout the UK and these provide an opportunity for people at all levels of experience to meet, exchange ideas and work on their own personal and professional development. The most prominent of these started life as the Paddington Group, meeting near Paddington station in central London in the 1990s. This group introduced a wide range of people to NLP and acted as a forum for prominent practitioners from the UK and outside.

The Association for Neuro-Linguistic Programming (ANLP)

Formed in 1985 as a non-profit making organization, the Association for Neuro-Linguistic Programming was, until recently, a registered educational charity, recognized internationally as probably the leading association for those interested in, and using, NLP. Originally set up by Eileen Whicker following an inaugural meeting at the London Business School on 8 May 1985, it was envisaged as an umbrella organization for the development of NLP; in Eileen's words, 'setting core standards for training and practice, being a basis for exchanging information and experience, creating links with other NLP bodies, setting standards and ethics, promoting research, keeping abreast of legislation and representing NLP in a professional capacity to Government and serving on the Steering Committees then being set up'.

The preparatory meeting held to form the Association was attended by Eileen Whicker, Eileen Watkins Seymour, Basil Jones, Dudley Masters, Valerie Beeby and Surya and John Watson. Support was also obtained from Eric Robbie and Willie Monteiro as well as Gene Early. A steering committee was then set up, consisting of Eileen Whicker, Nigel Gowland, Eileen Watkins Seymour and Roy Johnson, and the first meeting, on 12 April 1985, resulted in an open invitation being sent to other interested people.

The inaugural meeting was held at the London Business School on 8 May 1985 and around 60 people participated. The first executive committee consisted of: Chair: Eileen Whicker, Vice Chair: Peter Rust, Treasurer: Roy Johnson, Secretary: Regan Masters, Membership Secretary: Paul Clarke. Eric Robbie helped to prepare the Association's first newsletter and Frank Kevlin, later to become Chair, helped set up and print the first issue of *Rapport*, currently a quarterly magazine of international reputation.

From these beginnings, ANLP expanded to around 1,000 members in the late 1990s, worldwide, in all walks of life. After Eileen, Chairs of the Association were Frank Kevlin (who died very tragically at a young age), Sue Burke, Peter Child, Carol Harris and Derek Jackson. In 1996, the Psychotherapy and Counselling Section (PCS), which had existed for several years, became a wholly owned subsidiary company of ANLP, catering for those involved in therapeutic applications and leaving the main body of ANLP covering those in business, personal development work and a myriad of other activities, with its main activities being public information, recognition of training organizations, conference organization and magazine production.

Recently, PCS separated from ANLP, the Association's charitable status stopped and it ceased recognizing training organizations or courses. It is now simply an information and networking organization rather than a professional body. No longer a leading international entity, its future development is likely to be limited if it pursues its present path.

People

Let us now turn to some other people who were involved in NLP's development, contributed ideas which were seminal to its progress, or helped popularize and promote it as a field of activity.

Richard Bandler and John Grinder

As mentioned above, these two men are recognized as NLP's major co-founders. Although they are generally credited with 'creating NLP', many of its ideas and principles had come from earlier thinkers, or been based on their ideas and writings.

Alfred Korzybski

Recognized as the founding father of general semantics, Count Korzybski had a major effect on the development of NLP and, in particular, the 'Meta-Model' *(see Chapter 3)*.

Born in Warsaw in 1879, Korzybski trained as an engineer. He served in the First World War, attached to the General Staff Intelligence Department of the Second Russian Army, and later served in the US and Canadian military services, remaining in the USA from 1921. He developed his theory of time-binding around 1921 and published his first book, *Manhood of Humanity*, in 1921 and his most famous work, *Science and Sanity*, in 1933.

Korzybski was founder and Director of the Institute of General Semantics, which was established in 1938 as a centre for training in his work. One of its aims was 'neuro-linguistic' research and education. Korzybski was the first person to use the term 'neuro-linguistic' and it appeared in *Science and Sanity*; he continued to write and lecture until his death in 1950.

Noam Chomsky

Chomsky was a professor of linguistics whose work, based on Korzybski's earlier ideas, was key to much of the development of NLP. Now a revolutionary figure prominent in US politics, he became very anti-establishment at the time of the Vietnam War. Chomsky's work on general semantics first appeared in a range of published papers and culminated in the 1957 publication *Syntactic Structures* (now out of print). This work established the transformational model of language, with its concepts of deep structure and surface structure, elements which feature heavily in NLP's approach to precision in language. Chomsky's 1965 book *Aspects of Theory and Syntax*, published by MIT Press, is an easier publication for the general reader.

Gregory Bateson

Bateson was a British anthropologist and author who influenced several of NLP's leading proponents. His father, a geneticist who coined the word 'genetics', named him after the famous Russian geneticist Gregor Mendel.

Bateson wrote on a range of topics including communications, systems theory/cybernetics, psychology, psychiatry, anthropology, biological evolution and genetics. He received a Guggenheim Fellowship for his first attempts to synthesize cybernetic ideas with anthropological data. He was 'ethnologist' at the Veterans Administration Hospital at Palo Alto from 1949 until 1962. At the time he was married to Margaret Mead, another famous anthropologist, who also worked with him on many projects.

Later, Bateson's communication studies were extended to the animal kingdom and, together with his then wife, Lois, he kept about a dozen octopuses in their living-room! He went on to become director of a dolphin laboratory in the Virgin Islands, where he continued his studies on communications in animals for about a year. In 1963 he went to the Oceanic Institute in Hawaii to work on problems of animal and human communication and it was there that he wrote most of his book *Steps to an Ecology of Mind* (1972).

Bateson also led the Palo Alto Group (*see page 35*) and lectured at the University of Santa Cruz at the time that Bandler and Grinder were developing NLP. He was a neighbour of Bandler's and it was he who suggested that Bandler and Grinder visit Milton Erickson (*see Erickson, page 40*).

Bateson considered that ideas were not abstract concepts, but the basis for the way people live their lives. He said that people should think and act systemically, by allowing both conscious and unconscious processes to shape their decisions, and by developing congruity in diverse parts of the mind. In the preface to Bateson's *Steps to an Ecology of Mind*, Mark Engel says:

The central idea in this book is that we create the world that we perceive, not because there is no reality outside our heads ... but because we select and edit the reality we see to conform to our beliefs about what sort of world we live in ... For a man to change his basic, perception-determining beliefs ... he must first become aware that reality is not necessarily as he believes it to be.

Carlos Castaneda

An anthropologist and writer whose works greatly influenced Bandler and Grinder and their associates, Castaneda made great use of metaphor, often in conversational dialogues, and some of his ideas were to form the basis for therapeutic interventions. His thoughts on 'stopping the world' – a concept where the mind is stilled to allow expansion of consciousness – was one of the underpinning elements of New Code NLP (*see Chapter 3*).

Ross Ashby, Stafford Beer and Peter Checkland

These systems thinkers and writers have strongly influenced NLP. Ashby originated the Law of Requisite Variety in 1956, emphasizing that it is important to keep exploring variations when working towards results. The principle behind his theory is that, in any system, the part that has the most flexibility will predominate, and as a system becomes more complex, more flexibility is required. Beer provided models which can be used with both individuals and organizations, and Checkland was the developer of 'soft systems' thinking.

Albert Ellis

A psychotherapist, writer and lecturer whose work was a major influence on several people working in NLP, especially Robert Dilts and Judith DeLozier, Ellis felt that traditional therapy sessions were too long and tried a more active approach based on work by early philosophers. His technique – Rational-Emotive Therapy, or RET – was a synthesis of psychology and philosophy. It has been described as 'perhaps the most widely practised form of the cognitive-behavioural therapies' (Yankura and Dryden, *Doing RET: Albert Ellis in Action*, Springer Publishing Company, 1990). Ellis concentrated on an individual's beliefs and identified both rational and irrational beliefs during therapy; his work also incorporated shifts in time in a similar way to that employed by NLP *(see Chapter 3)*.

Roberto Assagioli

Assagioli is known as the founder of psychosynthesis, on which he published the seminal book in 1965. In recent years, his work has been rediscovered and Michael Hall, an American therapist and NLP trainer, has written of it in the American NLP publication *Anchorpoint*. Hall outlines several of Assagioli's ideas and exercises and shows that his work predated NLP by around ten years. Some areas of similarity include what NLP knows as 'Well Formed Outcomes' (objective setting), sub-modalities (elements of sensory perception), 'anchoring', 'swish techniques', 'personality parts' and spiritual development. Genie

Laborde names Assagioli as one of the possible sources for NLP in her book *Influencing with Integrity*.

Maxwell Maltz

Maltz was a plastic surgeon writing in the 1960s, again before NLP was 'created'. His book *Psycho-Cybernetics* contained ideas, references and guidance using numerous techniques which we now regard as NLP.

Paul Watzlawick

Austrian by birth, Watzlawick was a research assistant at the Mental Research Institute (MRI) in Palo Alto from 1960 and Clinical Associate Professor at the Department of Psychiatry and Behavioural Sciences at Stanford University Medical Center. He was later Professor of Psychotherapy at the University of El Salvador in central America. One of his books, *Change*, sets out many of his ideas, which were invaluable to the development of NLP.

Virginia Satir

As mentioned earlier, Satir was one of the earliest, and best-known, people whose ways of working acted as models for the analysis and development of many NLP principles and processes. She was a social worker who was particularly interested in family systems. She developed an approach to family therapy which she called 'conjoint family therapy' and taught the subject at the Mental Research Institute (MRI) in Palo Alto, in the first training programme in the country on family therapy.

One of Satir's ways of working was with what she termed 'parts parties', where people would act out the characteristics of different facets of personality. A model which is associated with her is her analysis of five different personality elements, which have become known as 'Satir categories'. She gave these categories the names of 'Blamer', 'Placator', 'Distractor', 'Computer' and 'Leveller'. Each can be recognized through typical postures and modes of communication. These patterns are discussed in her book *Peoplemaking*, published in 1972.

Satir was very innovative and used games, exercises, audio, video, one-way mirrors and demonstrations in her work, approaches which have since become commonplace but were at that time novel techniques. She was the first Director of Training at the famous Esalen Institute, which was at the forefront of the Growth Potential movement. It is said that she was deaf until the age of ten, so, like Erickson *(see page 40)*, with some sensory impairment, she developed her observation skills to an extraordinarily high degree. Fritz Perls described her as 'the most nurturing person known'. Satir died in 1988.

Fritz Perls

Like Satir, Perls was another of the best-known models for NLP's development. He is often credited as the founder of Gestalt Therapy, although three other people, including his wife, co-authored with him the first book on the subject. Gestalt psychology dated back to 1912, but Perls turned it into a therapeutic tool. The word 'Gestalt' refers to a pattern of parts which make up a whole and Gestalt psychology indicates that a study of parts alone is not sufficient to lead to understanding – the whole must be taken into account.

Born in Berlin in 1893, Perls gained an MD in psychiatry. Originally influenced by Freud, he rejected the psychoanalytic movement, believing that the present is more important than the past. Often blunt and ignoring conventional pleasantries, Perls encouraged his subjects to explore their emotional responses through processes including the use of 'hot seats' through which a person could exchange roles by moving to a different seat where they could act out a different part.

Perls emigrated to the USA in 1946, founded the New York Institute for Gestalt Therapy in 1952 and moved to California in 1959, becoming involved with Esalen, the Californian centre for the human-growth movement and associated therapy. He remained there until 1969, when he moved to Canada and founded the Gestalt Institute of British Columbia; he died in 1970, six months after it was established.

Milton Erickson

Erickson, also part of the trio of notable NLP role models, was born in 1901 in Aurum, Nevada. His parents were pioneers who travelled to their destination in a covered wagon. He was colour blind, perceiving the colour purple but little else. He was also tone deaf, dyslexic and had arrhythmia, an irregularity of the heart. He did not learn to speak until the age of four and, because of his breathing and hearing difficulties, had an unusual vocal pattern. He had two bouts of polio, the first at 17 years of age and the second when he was 51. Although he recovered almost completely from the total paralysis of the first bout, the second left him severely paralysed, initially in his legs, right arm and part of his left arm, and later affecting his diaphragm and mouth. He was frequently in pain, which he alleviated with daily self-hypnosis exercises.

Erickson was first a psychologist and later a medical doctor. He studied at the University of Wisconsin from 1921 to 1924 under Professor Clark L. Hull, who was a key figure in the development of clinical hypnosis and the subject of some controversy at the university, where he used students as part of his research into hypnotic processes. (Hull's seminal book on hypnosis, first published in 1933, is currently being rereleased by Crown House Publishing.) Hull appointed Erickson to lead a study group into hypnotic inductions and suggestibility, which is where he first encountered the subject.

Erickson completed his MD degree in 1928 and became Chief Psychiatrist at Worcester State Hospital in Massachusetts. He later became Director of Psychiatric Research and Psychiatric Training at Eloise Hospital and Infirmary in Eloise, Michigan, where he stayed until 1949, while also taking on professorships at other centres. In 1948 he moved to Phoenix, Arizona, mainly for health reasons, where he established a private practice and used his hypnotherapy skills to achieve extraordinary results. Later, he became founding President of the American Society of Clinical Hypnosis and founding editor of the *American Journal of Clinical Hypnosis.*

In later life, Erickson's fame spread and in his seventies he was publicly recognized for the hypnosis work for which in earlier years he had been condemned by the medical establishment. He had even been forbidden, while at the Colorado General Hospital as an intern, to mention the topic of hypnosis under the threat of dismissal and refusal of his state licence.

Erickson was divorced from his first wife and, in his two marriages, fathered eight children. As one of the subjects of Bandler and Grinder's studies, where his language and behaviour were examined in detail and many patterns defined, he provided the basis for much of what is now known as the 'Milton Model' *(see Chapter 3).* He made particular use of indirect language patterns and ways of gaining rapport with his clients, which became known as Ericksonian hypnosis (although his original work was with classical hypnosis and he only really developed his newer approach during the 1950s). He died in March 1980.

Frank Farrelly

A psychotherapist, trainer and author, Farrelly was Clinical Professor at the School of Social Work at the University of Wisconsin and was reported to have been involved with the Palo Alto Project. He is the developer of provocative therapy, which aims to bring about personal change through challenge and humour, and, together with Jeff Brandsma, authored the book *Provocative Therapy.*

Farrelly is funny, outrageous, irreverent and almost impossibly direct, while retaining respect for the subjects of his repartee. He has undoubtedly been a major role model for other well-known NLP figures, although his work is not specifically NLP-based. Richard Bandler apparently visited him in California and videoed his workshops for later study.

Farrelly's interests also include parapsychology, into which he has carried out research and about which he has many fascinating stories to tell.

Judith DeLozier

DeLozier's background was in religious studies and anthropology; she was also a music and dance teacher. Her involvement with NLP started when John Grinder, to whom she was married for some years, gave her a manuscript copy of *The Structure of Magic* to read and comment on. She became one of the co-founders of NLP and originated much of the early material; she was also co-developer, with Grinder, of New Code NLP *(see Chapter 3)*. She was introduced to hypnosis when Gregory Bateson suggested she work with Milton Erickson for a time. She specializes in epistemology (the theory of knowledge/study of how people know what they know) and cross-cultural applications of NLP.

Leslie Cameron Bandler

Cameron Bandler was a student of community studies (for which Santa Cruz was famous) and psychology. She was involved with the NLP group at the university and later became the first Research Director of the Society of NLP set up by Richard Bandler and John Grinder. Married for a year or so to Bandler (Grinder conducted the ceremony), she later married Michael LeBeau. Together with LeBeau and David Gordon, she set up an organization in Larkspur, California, called the Centre for Advanced Studies.

Cameron Bandler left the NLP world in the mid to late 1980s and became very involved in green campaigning in the USA.

David Gordon

A psychology student and one of the original group of co-developers of NLP, Gordon's approach is characterized by curiosity, humour, systematic thinking, originality and respect. Peppered with anecdotes, his training also makes liberal use of metaphor, a subject with which he is much engaged and which formed the basis of his master's degree thesis and, subsequently, one of his best-known books, *Therapeutic Metaphors*.

Gordon has made major contributions to the field of NLP including, with Leslie Cameron Bandler and Michael LeBeau, exploring the structure of subjective experience. Together they developed the Mental Aptitude Patterning (MAP) model, which further developed into the concept of the Imperative Self, a model which demonstrates what it is about a person which holds constant across contexts and time and is likely to be true from birth to death. Gordon was also the developer, with Graham Dawes, of the Experiential Array, possibly the least publicized major model of NLP. Another recent development of his has been the Meaningful Existence model, which he put together on the basis of observation of and discussion with people leading personally successful and rewarding lives. Gordon has also contributed much to the professional development of NLP in Britain as well as the USA, largely through his work as a trainer with the UKTC on its pioneering NLP courses.

Robert Dilts

Another of the early co-developers of NLP, Robert Dilts was a student at Santa Cruz and also studied with Bateson and Erickson. He is noted for his creative approach to NLP and for his continuing development of numerous models, the best known being the Neurological Levels model.

Fascinated by the study of people who excel in their fields, Dilts is author of a series of books on famous individuals, including Einstein, Walt Disney, Aristotle and Mozart. He also co-authored, with Grinder, Bandler and DeLozier, the standard NLP work *Neuro-Linguistic*

Programming: Volume 1, as well as publishing many other books. Other interests of his are NLP and spirituality and NLP and health, and he has told of his work with his mother, who had cancer and later made a full recovery.

Dilts is well known throughout the world for his training courses as well as being a trainer on the first NLP courses run in the UK by the UKTC. He was also the creator of what is probably the first degree course in NLP when he designed his own programme, which he called 'Human Engineering'.

Steve and Connirae Andreas

Steve Andreas's mother was Barry Stevens, who was a major figure in the Gestalt world and had a close relationship with Fritz Perls. Andreas himself lectured in Gestalt and related subjects at the University of Utah and edited *Gestalt Now*, a leading US magazine of the time. He knew Bandler before Bandler was involved in NLP, became interested in the work being carried out and, in 1978, gave up his Gestalt Therapy to work with NLP himself. He is the author, or co-author, of many books on the subject.

Connirae was a student of Steve's and later his wife. She was introduced to Bandler and Grinder by Steve in 1997/8 and, together with Steve, was responsible for tape-recording many of their workshops and turning them into some of the best-known NLP books around: *Frogs into Princes*, *Trance-formations* and *Re-framing*. They also wrote *Heart of the Mind* and have been active in developing new NLP change patterns and models of human excellence. Connirae is best known for her work on Core Transformation.

Todd Epstein

Epstein became involved with NLP in 1979, having served his apprenticeship with Bandler. He was a partner at the Dynamic Learning Center and the NLP University, a US training organization, with Dilts and

DeLozier. He co-authored several books with Dilts and worked closely with him on developing various NLP models. A great musician and famous for his storytelling, he died in 1995.

Terrence McClendon

McClendon was a student at the University of Santa Cruz at the same time as Bandler and Grinder and participated in many of the early NLP group activities. He has a master's degree in psychology and is a licensed counsellor. He is the author of *The Wild Days*, a highly personal account of NLP's emergence in California, and the developer of a personality assessment survey. He went to Australia in the 1970s and founded the Australian Institute of NLP.

Stephen Gilligan

Gilligan is an internationally recognized authority on Ericksonian therapy, a trainer and therapist. He studied with Gregory Bateson at the University at Santa Cruz and was involved in the conception of NLP, but left the field in 1977 when he considered it was becoming 'arrogant and fundamentalist – emphasizing techniques and evidences of programming rather than the meaning of our experience'.

Gilligan talks of there being different forms of NLP, some fundamentalist and some aesthetic. The fundamentalist approach 'emphasizes one right way and concentrates on an image and representational systems rather than what lies behind them'. However, he says, 'some people still approach it contextually as a first base', including Dilts and DeLozier (USA) and Julian Russell (UK). Gilligan's own approach, 'Self-Relations', concentrates on the relationships within individuals between the conscious and unconscious minds. The first self is the unconscious mind and the second self the conscious mind.

At one stage, as part of his attempts to model Erickson, Gilligan confined himself to a wheelchair, but abandoned it when Erickson feared he would develop unwanted symptoms and persuaded him to simply copy what he did, rather than who he was.

Wyatt Woodsmall

Woodsmall is a business consultant and management trainer. He was co-founder and President of the International NLP Trainers Association (INLPTA) and co-founder of the International NLP Business Alliance and is past President of the North American Association for NLP. He is also a Senior Vice-President of the International Research Institute for Human Typological Studies, where his main emphasis is on the connection between human differences and performance.

Woodsmall is best known for his work on behavioural modelling, including an exercise undertaken while working for the US Department of Defense. In that exercise, Woodsmall and a few others in his team (including Anthony Robbins), modelled some of the top pistol shots in the army and then trained a normal class of recruits. They produced excellent results compared with a test group which trained normally. More recently, Woodsmall and his wife worked with the US Olympic diving team and modelled some of the elite US divers. During the following Olympics, the US team won three medals, although they had not been expected to win any.

One of Woodsmall's students on a Master Practitioner course was Tad James, who went on to produce the book *Time Line Therapy and the Basis of Personality* with him. And, with Marvin Oka, Woodsmall extended time-line work into 'Time Codes' in the mid-1990s.

Tad James

James has a master's degree in communications, a PhD in Ericksonian hypnosis and was originally a business consultant. He is probably best known for his work with time lines and the co-creator, with Wyatt Woodsmall, of Time Line Therapy™ – a specific approach to resolving problems using hypnotic techniques in association with mental 'movement through time'. He also specializes in another, rather esoteric, doctrine – Hawaiian Huna, an ancient spiritual tradition which has become increasingly used in recent years. James has also run courses in Mesmerism, an almost forgotten and often misunderstood precursor to modern-day hypnosis. He is extremely knowledgeable about NLP and other fields of study, spending much time researching psychology, healing and Huna, as well as other topics. When in London he is a familiar visitor to the libraries and archives for which the city is famous.

Charles Faulkner

Faulkner studied with the original developers of NLP, his own field at the time being literature. He introduced Cognitive Linguistics to NLP, including the idea that individuals and organizations have a metaphor of identity through which they understand themselves and their world. He is the principal co-author of the audio programmes *NLP: The New Technology of Achievement* and *Success Mastery with NLP*, and co-author, with Steve Andreas, of the book *NLP: The New Technology of Achievement* and is noted for his NLP modelling of financial 'market wizards'.

Christina Hall

Hall is probably best known for her work on new patterns and concepts in language and research into the exploration of language production as a powerful catalyst for change. She attended a seminar run by Bandler and Grinder in 1977 and in 1981 Bandler invited her to train with him, which she did for six years. A frequent contributor to NLP training courses around the world, Hall also completed a master's programme in counselling and practised as a therapist for a time.

Anthony Robbins

Robbins has probably done more than anyone else to popularize NLP. At 6'7", and injecting as much energy into his presentations as a whole army of conventional trainers, he is a larger-than-life figure. An ex-salesman, he is famous for his large-scale events, involving several thousand people, at which he talks about sales, leadership and enhancing personal potential. He has produced many popular books and audiotapes about using NLP, the best known probably being his 1987 book *Unlimited Power*. He is possibly most noted for his courses, where, as a high spot of the final day, participants are encouraged to walk on hot coals, on the premise that if they can gain the personal confidence to do this, they can do anything.

Eric Jensen

Jenson is a leading writer and practitioner in the field of accelerated learning. In the 1950s there had been moves in different countries, including Israel and the USA, to explore what made excellent teachers stand out from those who did not achieve such good results. In the mid-1970s, Jenson came across Bandler and Grinder and did some training with Bandler. He became especially interested in how the use of modalities (different senses) impinged on the teaching process and his first book, *Super Teaching*, utilized NLP techniques in conjunction with teaching theory.

Gene Early

Apparently the first person to give workshops on NLP in Europe, Early was one of the founders of the UKTC in Great Britain. He had a background in Transactional Analysis (TA) therapy, trained with Bandler and Grinder and later became a Vice-Chancellor of the University of the Nations in Hawaii, a Christian mission organization.

Graham Dawes

A British trainer, Dawes came across NLP when doing a BA by independent study as a mature student. With the encouragement of his tutor, Ian Cunningham, he made NLP the focus of his degree. When visiting the US he met Gene Early and began an association which led to him meeting Eileen Watkins Seymour and becoming a founder director of the UKTC. He works closely with David Gordon, especially in the development of modelling processes, including the Experiential Dynamics model *(see Chapter 3)*.

Ian Cunningham, Roy Johnson, David Gaster and Barbara Witney

These are other trainers who were instrumental in the early development of NLP in the UK. Cunningham did a lot of early training at the UKTC and was the developer of self-managed learning. Gaster, who died at an early age, was well known in the USA and the UK and, before his involvement with NLP, was a flyer, taking part in acrobatic displays.-His work was largely in a business context and he also trained with the UKTC. Johnson was involved in many early NLP programmes, one of which was the first NLP workshop attended by the author of this book. Witney was also another regular US trainer with the UKTC in its early days.

Shelle Rose Charvet

Charvet, a Canadian, trained with Rodger Bailey, the developer of the Language and Behaviour (LAB) profile, a questionnaire which identifies people's use of Meta-Programmes. Charvet is a consultant and trainer specializing in the use of the LAB profile methodology. She is the author of *Words that Change Minds,* an excellent book on the use of Meta-Programmes in influencing. She has also produced a range of audiotapes and CDs on Meta-Programme applications.

Michael Hall

Hall has been a cognitive-behavioural psychologist, a researcher, modeller, international trainer and prolific writer. He studied with Bandler and wrote several books about Bandler's trainings. He discovered the *Meta-States* model while modelling resilience and subsequently developed the field of *Neuro-Semantics*.

David Grove

Grove conducts therapy based on the fact that people's experience is often conveyed through symbols – in words, gestures and other processes. He helps people explore how they use metaphor and metaphorical space around themselves through his process of 'cognitive mapping' and has developed the concept of 'clean language', a way of using entirely neutral language in order to avoid imposing the therapist's own perceptions upon the client. Although he has not published his work, the book *Metaphors in Mind*, by Penny Tompkins and James Lawley, is based on his approach.

This chapter has outlined the activities of several of the people who have been most influential in NLP. There are many more who cannot be mentioned here because of lack of space, but for those interested there is a wealth of further reading available, as well as the opportunity to attend workshops and training events at which many of these people present their ideas and work.

Chapter 3

Frameworks, Models and Techniques

Over the years, there has been a divergence of opinion about what constitutes NLP. For those not familiar with the field, NLP can seem like a collection of techniques and processes which, if used effectively, can produce extraordinary results. The popular press, in particular, have focused on those NLP processes which sound unusual or extraordinary, and this has often given the impression that NLP is quirky and just a collection of 'quick fixes'. However, it is really much more than its component parts; it provides a holistic and broad approach to the development of excellence which is not always apparent to those who concentrate exclusively on its specific and characteristic 'technology'.

Having said the subject is more than its parts, however, for those interested in how NLP enables people to achieve success, this chapter is devoted to outlining and exploring the models, framework and techniques which give NLP its particular character. Frameworks and models are not complete explanations of reality, but they do act as helpful guides to how people function. Techniques cannot be used in isolation; they need to be set in the context of the whole person and the whole situation. The breakdown into the different categories is somewhat arbitrary; in presenting some of the best-known models, frameworks and techniques, I have chosen to group the broader conceptual approaches as frameworks, the more specific ones as models and the ones with detailed practical applications as techniques, which I hope is relatively easy to follow.

Frameworks

The Experiential Array

The Experiential Array was developed by David Gordon (USA) and Graham Dawes (UK) as a joint project, beginning in 1987 and being refined, especially in the area of 'beliefs', until the present day. The array creates a framework for exploring the structure of effective performance and is, I believe, the simplest way of understanding what NLP does. At the time of writing, this model has not yet been published, although it has appeared in course material produced by David and Graham and they have, for some time, been working on a book on their developments.

In essence, the array has two applications: personal change and modelling/performance enhancement. It outlines five elements which contribute to performance:

★ outcomes
★ behaviour
★ mental strategies (thoughts)
★ emotional states (feelings)
★ beliefs and values

Each of these interrelates, so the whole forms a complete system, with the 'internal' elements of thinking and feeling affecting behaviour and behaviour affecting the results (outcomes) achieved. Because of these interrelationships, if one part of the system changes, it has an effect on others, creating changes in them also.

The diagram below represents the interrelation of these elements and also indicates the degrees of influence exerted by them on each other. So the relative size of the arrows indicates the degree of influence, with the impact of feelings and thoughts on behaviour being greater than the impact of behaviour on feeling and thinking. Similarly, beliefs have a greater impact on thoughts, feelings and behaviour than any of these have on beliefs at any given time. Over time, of course, these elements may contribute experiences which ultimately change beliefs.

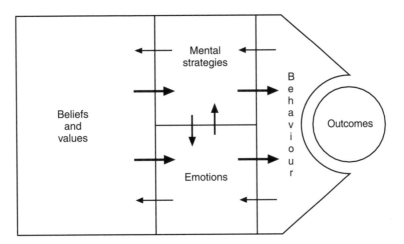

The Experiential Array

To use the array to make changes, a further element can be added – a 'desired outcome' circle. It is then possible to work out which of the other elements (behaviour, thoughts, feelings or beliefs and values) needs to be varied or developed in order to achieve that desire.

As context is important, the five elements may vary from situation to situation. So, for example, a person may have one kind of behaviour at work (one context) and a different kind of behaviour at home (different context). Also, within the same context, different people may have widely different thoughts, feelings, behaviour, beliefs and objectives.

So this framework illustrates the process by which a person achieves results in a particular area. If a different result (outcome) is desired, then something needs to be changed within the system. In looking at the array, it is easy to see why a saying popular in NLP is true: 'If you always do what you've always done, you always get what you've always got.' The array shows how, if we utilize the same ways of thinking and acting, we get the same results, and also shows that if we make changes in these areas, we can develop and progress.

Neurological Levels (sometimes called 'Logical Levels')

This very well-known approach to NLP integrates various aspects of the subject into one framework which helps in thinking about learning, change and personal development. It was inspired by Gregory Bateson and developed by Robert Dilts. Bateson identified four levels of learning and change, with each level 'more abstract than the level below it but each having a greater degree of impact on the individual' (Dilts).

The framework has six basic levels at which an individual can be 'operating'; in ascending order they are:

★ environment (where and when things happen; opportunities and constraints)
★ behaviour (what a person does; actions and reactions)
★ capability (how a person does things, the skills utilized; the strategy and plans followed)
★ belief (why a person does things; what motivates them)

★ identity (who a person thinks they are; the sense of self and personal mission)

★ spirituality (what a person does things for; what exists beyond themselves)

These levels are considered to be a hierarchy, with spirituality at the top and environment at the bottom, each level 'involving more of an individual's neurology'. The levels are sometimes depicted as nested circles, but more often as triangles, with the first five levels as the base triangle and the higher levels as an inverted triangle above, as shown.

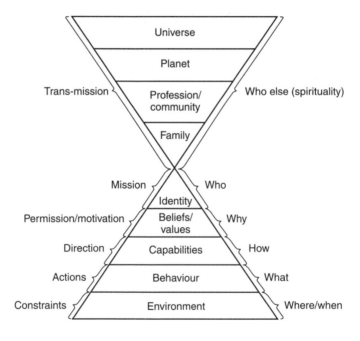

The framework can be used in a variety of ways, one being to check for consistency (congruence) between each level. For example, a person might think it important to be on time for meetings but, in practice, often be late, so the belief (timeliness is important) is contradicted by the behaviour (lateness). The framework helps people check whether what they think and do lines up with their self-identity and values. Inconsistency or conflict between these areas can lead to stress, misunderstanding by others and poor performance.

It is useful to use this framework on occasions when a person is functioning at an inappropriate level in the hierarchy. For example, someone might say: 'I couldn't [belief] wear earrings. I'm not the sort of person [identity] who could do that.' What you wear is behaviour, but the person has escalated the significance of the earrings to the level of personal identity, to the extent that wearing earrings can become a threat to their persona. By helping a person understand where their response is actually located in the logical levels hierarchy, it is possible to promote greater self-awareness and development.

The framework can also be applied to organizations. Suppose an organization calls in a consultant to advise on customer care, questions relating to the Neurological Levels framework can help identify any inconsistencies in what is happening. For example, the workplace may give an impression of untidiness (environment) and staff may not listen well to customers' views (behaviour); both of these could be at odds with an organizational opinion (belief) that paying attention to the customer is important. It may also be the case that the staff's beliefs about customer care do not correspond with those of the senior management, leading to mixed messages being given to customers or visitors.

Time Lines

This is a conceptual framework which deals with the ways in which people perceive themselves in relation to time and shows that people store time-based information in different ways.

The idea of time lines goes back a long way. Tad James, one of the leading people working in this area, has said that the ancient Greeks talked of the continuum of time in a way which is not dissimilar to current concepts; he has also mentioned that psychologist William James, writing in 1890 in *Principles of Psychology*, referred to time as having 'locations', saying, 'The present is a saddle-back on which we sit perched, and we look in two directions in time; location in space corresponds to time. We date a memory simply by tossing it in a certain direction.'

Time-line theory involves the concept that people 'organize' and react to time in different ways. To take a simple example, time often goes slowly when it seems uncontrollable (for example while waiting in a traffic jam) and passes rapidly during enjoyable events. Time therefore is not a fixed concept, but one which varies according to our perception of it. In his book on the nature of time E. T. Hall discusses how it is possible to alter perception of time deliberately and I will be covering his ideas on this subject in Chapter 6. It is also possible to alter perception of time through hypnosis, but these techniques are beyond the scope of this book.

NLP takes the concept of time further and makes it possible to imagine ourselves at different points in time and at different 'places' in relation to it. To illustrate this, one can imagine a line on the floor, one end of which represents the past and the other the future, with the present somewhere between. It is then possible to stand on the line at the spot which equates to the present time, look towards the future and imagine how it could be (for example seeing oneself carrying out a particular activity or having achieved a particular result). It is also possible to look back at the past in the same way to recall how one behaved then. Doing this visualization can help clarify one's feelings about certain events and occurrences. It is also possible to move physically backwards and forwards along the line as if one were revisiting the past or moving into the future. From these points it becomes relatively easy to access or reaccess the feelings which relate to the events concerned. Once 'immersed' in these events, it is possible to evaluate them from a different standpoint (literally), learn about one's responses and make appropriate changes.

Another way in which NLP considers time is in connection with people's 'orientation' in time. There are two basic orientations, although there are many other possible permutations. The first is what is called 'In Time', which means that a person is so immersed in their present experience that past, present and future seem to merge; such a person is often unaware of time passing and may be a poor time manager. The opposite orientation is called 'Through Time', which means that a person can 'see' time in front of them, instead of being immersed in it. In this case the person will be very aware of the significance of periods of time, have a good sense of how long activities are taking and generally be a good time manager. I will be covering this in more depth in Chapter 6.

The concept of time lines, really a metaphorical way of working with the topic, provides an excellent method of working through issues, getting different perspectives and developing greater personal control.

Unified Field Theory

Many people have thought about ways of integrating the whole of NLP into one framework. Robert Dilts has produced one such framework. He says that Albert Einstein 'sought a "unified field theory" for physics, which would tie together all physical theories into a single model of how the universe operated'. He also says: 'Neuro-Linguistic Programming began as a unified field theory – an operational framework that synthesized the fields of neurology, linguistics and artificial intelligence.'

Dilts says that, as NLP progressed, it moved away from the systemic model and towards linear 'step-by-step' approaches. He believes that although this has led to rapid transfer of skills and techniques, it has resulted in the loss of a 'bigger picture', so that many students of NLP struggle to understand how the tools and techniques they have learned fit together.

In order to overcome this, Dilts has devised a framework for understanding human performance. It has three elements:

★ levels of functioning (neurological levels)
★ time
★ perspective (perceptual positions)

The framework also addresses generative processes, ie ones which promote evolution and growth. Dilts says:

Generative NLP helps people solve problems and achieve goals in a more systemic and organic way. When new resources are created and developed, problems that are ready to be solved by those resources emerge and resolve naturally and without effort.

Dilts' integrating framework helps people 'develop elegance in managing the multiple levels and multiple perspectives of change and communication'. By learning how to operate within multidimensional 'spaces', people can achieve objectives through selecting the most appropriate courses of action to take. The diagram shows how Dilts has conceived interrelationships between the three elements of neurological (or logical) levels, perceptual positions and time.

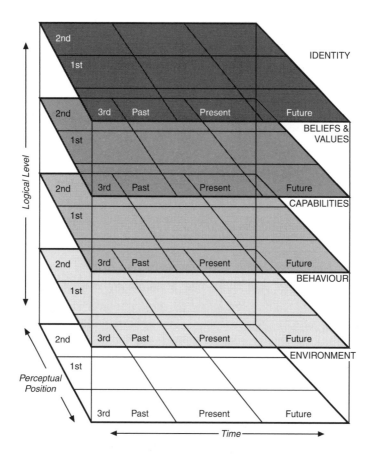

These elements have also been referred to as the 'Jungle Gym' and represented diagrammatically as a matrix with various 'boxes'. It has also, apparently, been built as a climbing frame which can be used in a physical way to explore the connections and experiences involved.

New Code NLP

New Code is a holistic way of approaching human potential and the book *Turtles All the Way Down* by John Grinder and Judith DeLozier, written in 1987, is an exposition of some of its ideas. New Code grew out of Gregory Bateson's work with information theory and biology, and Carlos Castaneda's books, as well as Grinder and DeLozier's experience of Native Americans, African drumming, dancing, singing and anthropological studies. Some of its approaches include active dreaming, the development of intuition and what are called 'personal edits', including the 'Alphabet Edit', attributed to John Grinder, which is a series of exercises designed to integrate left and right-brain activity.

Part of New Code is about the body's own ability to act as a feedback mechanism and the New Code approach teaches that by listening to the body, which has its own inborn wisdom, it is possible to obtain excellent information about what is or is not appropriate action to take. This can also be expressed as the process of conscious-unconscious dialogue. Roz Carroll (*Rapport* [ref. to come]) has said that: 'New Code increases the ability to take in information at all levels of being and to access it more easily!' and she quotes Judith DeLozier as saying that: 'New Code thinking took us out of technology and into relational and spiritual aspects of naturally occurring relationships.'

New Code has not been outlined in a structured way, perhaps because its very approach assumes an integrated and holistic way of functioning. A good description of it may be found in the transcript of a presentation by DeLozier to the Paddington Group in London in 1993, where she describes the difference between New Code and the existing NLP approaches. (The transcript was subsequently edited by James Lawley in the Swiss periodical *NLP World*, vol. II, no. 1, 1995. *NLP World* is no longer in production.) The following is a summary of this presentation.

'Old coding', or traditional NLP, arose from linguistics, Gestalt Therapy and systems theory. These disciplines produced the NLP language patterns and showed how they connected with the deep structure of experience. This in turn yielded the ideas of representational systems, sub-modalities, strategies, separating intent from behaviour and the techniques which followed on from these elements. Connections were made between the patterns of physiology, language and internal state. So traditional NLP explored structures of experience, the ways in which these structures are expressed in language and techniques for analysing and working with people's personal experience.

However, according to DeLozier, people were:

... viewing NLP as technology, as a procedure which I call a ritual. There is no wisdom in a piece of technology. Wisdom has to be in the carrier of that information. John Grinder and myself [sic] thought, 'How are we going to get people to start thinking about where is the wisdom?' and that is how Turtles All the Way Down: Prerequisites to Personal Genius *got written in 1984.*

New Code NLP provided a way for the inherent wisdom of the body to be acknowledged and utilized and Grinder and DeLozier defined New Code as containing the following elements:

1. **State** This is about developing an appropriate state in which to enhance excellence. One of the elements here is what Castaneda called 'stopping the world', a very clear state where internal dialogue is turned off, vision shifted from the centre to the periphery and tension allowed to dissipate.
2. **Conscious-unconscious relationship** This is about having a highly developed quality relationship between conscious and unconscious resources and knowing when to use the 'tight thinking of the cognitive conscious mind' and when to use the 'loose thinking of the more creative unconscious mind'. This is also to do with perceptual positions and the ability to shift in and out of detached perspectives on oneself.
3. **Balance between practice and spontaneity** This is similar to the previous point and is about allowing oneself to let go of deliberate activity and just 'be'. An example DeLozier gives is of the martial art Aikido, saying that after practising and practising, there comes a time when you just act – not deliberating what to do, but just doing.

4. **Perceptual position** This is about the fact that shifting positions allows us different perspectives on a situation. If you imagine watching yourself interacting with another person, you can begin to understand the part you both play in maintaining the interaction, for better or worse, and what you could do to enhance it. DeLozier says: 'The idea of perceptual positions is that, out of this dance of multiple perspectives, wisdom may begin to unfold. To really consider the movement from my personal map to an understanding of your personal map, and then to an objective position of the relationship, gives us a basis of wisdom.'

5. **Attention** Where you place your attention defines the quality of your perception; by paying tightly focused attention to one aspect, you may ignore others. If you find that fixing your attention on one aspect of an interaction leads you to a negative value judgement, you may choose to move your attention to another part and thereby notice if the quality of the interaction becomes more positive.

6. **Filters** Everyone perceives things selectively according to their experience and conditioning. By asking what filters you can let go of, you can push back your personal boundaries and experience even more. As DeLozier says, 'It's a question of … saying: "What sorts of arrangements can I make in my life to move myself to the edge so the surrounding unknown becomes available?"'

7. **Multiple descriptions** This is about widening our range of definitions so that instead of having just one approach to an issue, we can broaden our response to it.

Systemic NLP

Although not a single discrete framework, the systemic approach to NLP is concerned with relationships and interactions. Instead of isolating component parts of a system and looking at them as discrete units, the systemic approach shows how the whole can become more than the sum of its parts and how one part of a system can impinge on, and interact with, another. Robert Dilts says that New Code and Systemic NLP:

... were both developed in order to refocus NLP back onto its original roots. Their purpose has been to help NLP become more 'code congruent' with its presuppositions and the legacy of those individuals who served as its initial role models. The mission of systemic NLP and NLP New Coding is to reintroduce a cybernetic framework and bring systemic thinking skills into the practice of NLP.

The frameworks outlined above are some of the best known in NLP, although others do exist and are being developed on a continuous basis. We will now turn to some of the models which NLP uses in order to help understand and work with behaviour and change.

Models

A model may be described as a representation of a system or process, a representation which shows the component parts and how they interrelate. The first part of this section contains a model for achieving objectives; the second part contains a series of models on problem solving and creativity; the third part contains the best-known NLP language models.

'Modelling' is a term much used in NLP and it has a number of possible definitions. Probably the most common is that of a process whereby someone either analyses or copies (or both) another person's ways or patterns of behaving, thinking or reacting.

As an example of behavioural modelling, you could find that one neighbour always cuts the grass by walking up and down in straight lines, while another moves in decreasing circles; you could then copy (model) each in turn and notice which works best for you.

There are two different types of modelling within NLP. The first is what can be termed Deep-Trance Identification. This is carried out through 'absorbing' another person's characteristics by spending time immersed in observation and assimilation of their behaviour. The word 'trance' is used because the state in which this absorption of the other person's behaviour takes place is one of total focus (often in an 'unconscious' manner) on the subject.

The second kind of modelling is called strategy modelling. This process (first presented in the book *Neuro-Linguistic Programming: Volume 1*) involves a conscious exploration of the elements involved in a person's performance. The Experiential Dynamics framework *(see 'Experiential Array' see page 53)* utilizes this process. With strategy modelling it is possible to analyse and codify an individual's objectives, behaviour and ways of thinking and feeling; this analysis can be as detailed as required including, for example, tiny sub-elements of thinking (sub-modalities) such as the size and shape of images people visualize, the precise locations of feelings in their body and the precise breakdown of their behaviour, such as the position they sit in while making a telephone call or the colour ink they select to sign their letters. It is worth remembering that in modelling, the most elegant approach is to model simply the elements which make the *difference* between average performance end excellent performance; it is not necessary to model absolutely everything the person being modelled does.

Objective Setting
Well-Formed Outcomes
The NLP approach to working towards objectives is called the 'Well-Formed Outcomes' model (WFO for short). It is the starting-point for most NLP work, as the definition of a clear and achievable desired result is key to achievement. *(For more details of this model see Chapters 1 and 6.)*

Problem Solving and Creativity

TOTE

This model was developed by George Miller, Eugene Galanter and Karl Pribram and was first proposed in their book *Plans and the Structure of Behaviour* in 1960. It shows a feedback mechanism which can be used as an aid to problem solving, creativity and development.

The TOTE model assumes that, as we go about our daily lives, we rely on a process of feedback to inform our decisions. Feedback mechanisms are very common in automated processes and NLP applies the feedback concept to performance, showing that if we are not achieving a desired result, we need to take further action in order to succeed.

The TOTE has three elements that follow an initial 'input':

T = *Test*
O = *Operate*
E = *Exit*

The term 'TOTE' has four letters, as the 'test' stage may be repeated, as I will explain now.

If we take the example of starting a car, the engine needs to be switched on before the car can move. The 'test' is: 'Is the engine switched on?' If it is, the car can start and the person can 'exit' from that procedure. If the engine is *not* switched on, something needs to happen – an 'operation'. By turning the key, the engine starts. The 'test' can then be repeated: 'Is the engine switched on?' The answer this time is 'Yes' and so the person can now exit, having tested, operated and tested again before exiting.

The process assumes a goal, or outcome, and a variety of ways of achieving that goal. By trying out different approaches, the goal can be reached.

Translating the TOTE to interpersonal relations, a typical process could be as follows:

'Is the shop assistant being helpful to me?' (test)
'No.' (therefore no exit)
'What could I do differently? How about smiling?' (operate)
'Is the assistant being helpful now?' (test again)
'Yes.' (OK, exit)

The TOTE helps people evaluate what they are doing and be more flexible in order to achieve good results. The diagram shows this process in action.

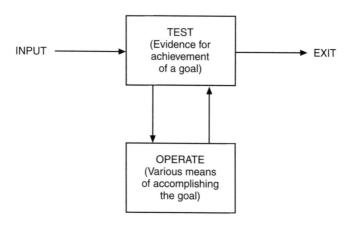

The cycle of 'Test ⟶ Operate' can be conducted as
many times as necessary in order to achieve the result.

ROLE

Another model developed by Robert Dilts, ROLE helps identify how people think, and consequently behave. It analyses mental strategy in relation to four factors:

★ Representational systems: Which of the senses – sight, sound, touch, taste, smell – does the person use most for the particular stage in their thinking?

★ Orientation: Is the person orientated internally – towards memories or imagination – or externally – towards the outside world?

★ Linkage: How is one step in the strategy linked to the others in a sequence? Do different stages overlap or are they sequential?

★ Effect: What is the effect, result or purpose of the step in the strategy? For example, to access, organize, evaluate or judge information?

By considering each of these elements, it is possible to map a person's thought experience and then help them become more flexible, creative and effective, if that is what they desire.

Dilts says the ROLE model can be made into a BAGEL by checking the following:

★ Body posture
★ Accessing cues (breathing, facial expression, etc)
★ Gestures
★ Eye movements
★ Language patterns

These elements are necessary either to put a thought process into action (application) or to check how a person is actually thinking (identification).

SCORE

This model, developed by Robert Dilts and Todd Epstein between 1987 and 1991, has to do with creative problem solving and proposes that there are five elements involved in this process:

★ Symptoms – 'the most noticeable and conscious aspects of a problem state; remaining fairly constant over time'

★ Causes – 'underlying elements responsible for creating and maintaining symptoms; tending to be less obvious than symptoms'

★ Outcomes – 'desired states or goals that take the place of symptoms'
★ Resources – 'elements responsible for transforming causes and symptoms and creating and maintaining outcomes or effects'
★ Effects – 'responses to, or results of, achieving an outcome; they may be positive or negative in how they affect motivation'

The five elements interrelate and can be assessed and handled in different ways in order to achieve a solution.

The Disney Strategy

This is slightly different from the preceding models, as it has been developed from the observation of one individual. Much of NLP is about 'role modelling' others in order to find out how they get results and then help others achieve similar results through transfer of the skills involved. The Disney Strategy is based on Walt Disney and is outlined in the books *Tools for Dreamers* by Robert B. Dilts, Todd Epstein and Robert W. Dilts (father of Robert) and *Skills for the Future* by Robert Dilts with Gino Bonissone. The strategy is a representation of how Disney achieved some of his creative results.

Dilts says that people were often puzzled by Disney, as he often seemed to shift from one way of behaving to another. He codified Disney's behaviour and found it fell into three distinct elements, which he called 'the Dreamer', 'the Realist' and 'the Critic'. The Dreamer 'generates the initial conceptual formulation of the idea'. The Realist 'carries out the task of implementing the idea in a tangible form'. The Critic (called 'the Spoiler' by Disney's associates) 'is the evaluator ... the one that really turns something into a valuable contribution'.

Each of these 'states' seems to have its own characteristic posture and thought processes. For example, the Dreamer can be represented looking up, being relaxed, focusing on the broad picture and thinking that anything is possible; the Realist can be represented looking ahead, leaning forward, considering short-term actions and assuming results are achievable; the Critic can be represented as looking down, asking questions and thinking about what to do if problems occur.

Dilts proposed that using these three states could help in creativity and problem solving and went on, in his writing, to show how this could be developed further. This model is an excellent exposition of how to do behavioural modelling and provides a useful way of understanding, and teaching, creative processes.

Language Models

There are a range of language models in NLP; the best known are probably the Meta-Model and the Milton Model.

The Meta-Model

This model was developed by Richard Bandler and John Grinder and first published in book form as *The Structure of Magic: Volume 1*. It is a framework for understanding how people use language and how the use of language relates to other facets of experience.

The Meta-Model is about precision and understanding and offers ways of analysing specific elements of language to aid personal interaction. It is grounded in the work of earlier linguists, such as Chomsky and Korzybski *(see Chapter 2)* and is concerned with how language is simply an external demonstration of internal experience. It considers that language is a 'surface' structure which represents 'deep' structure, or experience itself. Language is not reality, it simply represents reality, and by being clear about the meaning of a person's language, it is possible to better understand that person's actual experience.

There are a number of elements in the model, but in essence it focuses on three points – points which can lead to confusion and misunderstanding. They are:

- ★ deletion
- ★ distortion
- ★ generalization

In other words, people do not always say exactly, or completely, what they mean, but leave things out, change them or turn them into broad categories rather than specific points. If you were to say 'I always love going out with friends', the statement sounds quite specific. However, there may be some places you do not like going to with friends; there may be some friends you like seeing for short times but get bored with quickly and there may be some times when you actually dislike going out with friends (for example when there is the last part of a riveting serial on television). So your statement is not invariably true or actually factually correct; it is simply a broad statement of your attitude towards an activity.

Now this is actually a good thing for, if we were to be absolutely precise about everything we said we would be very pedantic and conversations would be interminable. The Meta-Model, however, allows us to question communications which may be ambiguous, vague or insufficiently detailed, in the furtherance of better understanding. It also allows us to enhance our own communication by being clearer and more precise. Some examples are as follows:

Statement: *'I did very well in the exams.'*
Meta-Model question: *'Exactly how well?'*
Aim: *To clarify the level of performance.*

Statement: *'It's bad to be late.'*
Meta-Model question: *'Why is that?'*
Aim: *To find out the person's beliefs about lateness.*

Statement: *'Tidiness is important.'*
Meta-Model question: *'Who says so?'*
Aim: *To find out where the person's beliefs about tidiness came from.*

Statement: *'Everyone has problems with public speaking'*
Meta-Model question: *'Absolutely everyone?'*
Aim: *To show the statement is a generalization and allow the person to rethink.*

So, the Meta-Model is concerned with precision, clarity and mutual understanding. There is far more to the model than we are able to cover here and if you would like to find out more, it would be useful to read *The Structure of Magic* which, although not always entirely clear, or easy to read, is the best way of finding out how the developers of the model generated their ideas. Another early book on this topic is *Precision* by Michael McMaster and John Grinder.

The Milton Model

This model is also concerned with language but is, in many ways, the converse of the Meta-Model. While the Meta-Model is concerned with precision, the Milton Model is concerned with indirect language, which can be used very effectively to influence people.

The Milton Model is based on the language patterns of Milton Erickson *(see Chapter 2)*. Erickson was a master of communication, using language creatively and flexibly to achieve results with his patients. Although some people have said he was not always consciously aware of the processes he was using, when he was studied by Bandler and Grinder, distinctive patterns emerged, mainly found in his later work *(see brief biography in Chapter 2)*. Some of these patterns were codified and are now known as the Milton Model.

Some features of the Milton Model are its use of generalization, ambiguity, indirect language and suggestion. In considering the Meta-Model above, we found that its purpose was clarity and precision; why then is there a place for the direct opposite of this? The answer to this is that, at times, being non-specific in communication allows the other person to use their imagination, which can lead to creative thought and accessing of the unconscious mind. The use of suggestion can also lead to change in a non-directive manner.

Let's take an example to illustrate these two points. Suppose a friend asks your advice on buying clothes. Knowing they often select inappropriate garments, you might use Milton Model language to help them, while not being too prescriptive. You might say something along the following lines (the words in bold are indirect suggestions and the words in bold capitals are non-specific words):

*You might like to **consider** something **DRAMATIC**, possibly a **BRIGHTER** colour than you usually wear, with a **BOLD** design. You could **think about something different**, and maybe **go to a new designer** whose clothes are **RIGHT FOR YOUR LIFESTYLE.***

There are many more elements to the Milton Model and I will take one final one here. This is the use of language to shift a person's thinking into different time frames. This might include taking them back into the past to explore or gain a different perspective on events which have occurred. Probably a more common use, however, is that of shifting someone into the future (metaphorically) by using the future tense. So, for example, if a person is finding it difficult to start a task, you could say: 'When you've finished that, I think you'll be really pleased and feel good about having done it.' This implies that there will be a time when the task has been completed and also begins to allow the person to create for themselves the feeling they will get when the task has been done.

A simple shift to the future tense becomes both a confidence boost and a motivating process.

If you are interested in learning more about the Milton Model, there are many books available, as well as transcripts of Erickson's own work and videos of him in action. Some of these sources are listed in the Bibliography.

Techniques

We can now move to some of the techniques which NLP offers for enhancing awareness, developing flexibility and bringing about change. Numerous techniques are in existence and being developed; here some of the best known and most used.

Perceptual Positions

People often use phrases which refer to positions, such as 'If I were in your position' or 'I can see your point of view.' However, it is not always as easy to really understand how another person thinks, feels and acts. Perceptual positions offer ways of making such shifts of perspective.

NLP refers to a whole series of 'perceptual positions'. There are two basic ones and a range of additional ones. 'First position' describes a person's own way of being; if a person is 'in first position' they are very much grounded in their own body and often subject to strong emotional feelings. In contrast, being 'in second position' is about being detached and able to observe oneself from a different perspective. NLP calls the experience of being 'in first position' being *associated* and being 'in second position' being *dissociated* (*see diagram*).

'ASSOCIATED'   'DISSOCIATED'

First position   Second position
(where you are now)   (imagining watching
                             yourself from a distance)

In the associated state, one's experiences may be heightened. It is possible to relive past experiences 'as if one were still there' and to imagine future experiences in a similar way. The disadvantages of being associated are that it may be difficult to manage, or critically review, one's feelings and it is possible to feel submerged by emotions, which can be a problem, especially if past traumatic events are very much alive in one's imagination.

In the dissociated state it is possible to adopt a more detached view and to be able to monitor what one does as one does it; the disadvantage is that it can cut off emotional response and give the impression of being rather cold and distant.

Beyond first and second positions are a series of additional perspectives called 'meta-positions' as they relate to positions beyond the original ones. Sometimes the next position ('third position') is called 'a helicopter view' because in this position both the individual and any others with whom they are interacting can be observed at the same time. It is possible then to take on additional positions where one is 'watching oneself watching oneself'. Although third position has been called an observer position, one writer (Sinclair) has suggested that, by virtue of observing, the third person is, in effect, part of the situation and not beyond it at all and that true meta-positions are beyond third position, not just beyond second position.

An example of these positions is shown in the diagram, where a customer is in a shop.

In circle 1 the customer is queuing up to be served (first position).
In circle 2 an assistant is helping the customer (second position).
In circle 3 another person is waiting in line behind the customer and observing the other two (third position).

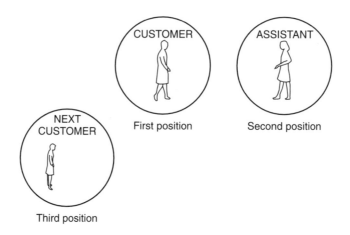

Shifting perspective can aid self-awareness, help understanding of other people's perspectives and make it possible to step back from one's emotions and review them in a more detached manner.

Reframing

This technique also deals with shifts of perception.

'Reframing' means simply to put another possible meaning on an event, a thought, a feeling or an act. As an example, a sore throat may be thought of as a nuisance; it could, however, be 'reframed' as an opportunity to rest or a chance to think and solve problems. By thinking of it in a different way, it is possible to be more positive and make the most of the situation.

People can reframe events for themselves or help others to reframe their own thoughts and experiences. Reframing can be used in a variety of contexts, including therapy, business and personal growth.

Chunking

This technique, borrowed from information technology, is also, in some ways, about shifts of perspective. By considering a situation from different levels, it is possible to gain insights into how to deal with it.

One way of thinking about a situation is to consider its component parts. The terms used here are 'chunking up' (thinking what lies beyond the issue being considered) and 'chunking down' (thinking what the component parts of an issue are). It is also possible to consider the 'chunks' on either side of an issue, in other words the elements which run parallel to it *(see Chapter 6 for an illustration of this process)*.

A further way of thinking about chunking is to consider how a large task or activity can be broken down into small parts ('small chunks') in order to become more manageable. An example often given is: 'You can eat an elephant if you cut it up into small enough bits first.' The process can be reversed and 'large chunks' considered if a person is being limited by going into unnecessary detail on a topic.

Excellent results can be achieved by helping people consider appropriate chunk sizes in what they are doing. Some applications here are time management (take small tasks at a time) and reading (get an overview first – 'large chunk' – then read the small print – 'small chunk').

Anchoring

This technique helps to create different responses through the use of association. It is grounded in the behaviourist approach to learning, which teaches that responses can be 'conditioned' by association.

An early example of this approach was Pavlov, whose work with dogs became world famous, the dogs learning to salivate when they heard a bell which had been rung as their food had been provided. Later, the bell alone produced a similar salivatory response. The process is like the experience of hearing a particular tune and finding it brings back a memory, or smelling a particular food and remembering where you were the first time you ate it.

'Anchoring' involves associating a trigger (or stimulus) with a response. So, for example, touching a person's shoulder when they are smiling can lead them, in the future, to feel good when touched again in a similar way. Similarly, a negative tone of voice, used frequently, can trigger the expectation of criticism.

Anchors may come in a variety of forms: simple ones, such as a touch or a sound, and more complex ones involving movement or chains (sequences) of linked anchors, each one leading the person into a further state of emotional response.

Anchoring is useful in helping a person to stay in a positive emotional state (for example calmness or cheerfulness) and can be used to good effect in therapeutic situations.

Richard Bandler has defined anchoring as 'the pairing of a stimuli [sic] with a highly predictable set of responses' (R. Bandler and J. LeValle, *Precision Engineering*, Meta Publications Inc., 1996).

Parts

Another technique which can be helpful in understanding confusion, solving problems and resolving conflict is the use of 'parts'. The term 'parts' is really metaphorical, relating to the fact that people often talk as if they were more than one entity. For example a person might say: 'Part of me wants to change jobs, but another part thinks it would be better to stay where I am.'

It is possible to use this concept to help a person come to terms with the differing elements of their personality. One way of doing this is to get them to talk about these personality elements as if they were embodied (ie had a physical presence and personality). Often, when a person talks about different parts, they will gesture in particular directions, for example to the left for one part and to the right for another. It is then possible to work with this representation and talk as if the parts were actually visible to the left or right and, if appropriate, get the person to say what size and shape each part is, what they look like, how they move, how they sound and so forth. By treating the parts as if they had individual personalities it is possible to work with them as if they were real, helping the person to understand what their roles are and how they can be utilized or changed if necessary.

Many of the applications of parts work are in therapy.

Sensory Preferences

Individuals vary in their use of the senses of sight, hearing, touch, taste and smell. Some people are very 'visual', others are more 'auditory' (concerned with language, sounds and 'internal dialogue'), others 'kinaesthetic' (relying heavily on their feelings). Some people use their senses of taste (gustatory) and smell (olfactory) to a high degree. NLP has various ways of working with sensory preferences. This is an area for which it is noted, yet it is really a very small part of what it can offer.

An initial way of working with sensory preferences is to assess the sensory channels that people are using. This includes the observation of body posture, gesture and eye movements, and speed of speech. For example, people tend to look up to visualize and look down when they are experiencing strong feelings. Visual people tend to speak quickly, as their speech is having to keep up with rapidly produced mental images, whereas kinaesthetic people tend to speak slowly, as feelings are often slow to access. Noticing these patterns helps to identify the sensory channels people are using.

Another useful process is to be able to identify people's sensory preferences through the words they are using; this can lead to being able to communicate more effectively with and influence people using appropriate words. This will be covered in more detail in Chapter 5.

As an example of language that relates to different senses, a visual person might use phrases such as 'I see', 'I can picture that', 'It looks good'; an auditory person might say 'It sounds good', 'That strikes a chord'; a person using internal dialogue (a sub-set of auditory) might say 'I think that's a good idea', 'It's in my mind to agree'; a kinaesthetic person might say 'I feel weighed down by that', 'It's a bit deep for me', 'Run that past me again'; a gustatory person might say 'I find that hard to swallow' and an olfactory person might say 'I'm on the scent of something new.'

There are many applications for sensory awareness. For example, Robert Dilts has developed a strategy for teaching spelling which relies on the use of visualization to assist in the process of perceiving and remembering the structure of words and Sid Jacobson works with people with dyslexia to help them manage their sensory responses when reading.

Sub-modalities

'Sub-modalities' is the term given to the distinctions made between aspects of sensory awareness. In addition to sight, hearing, touch, taste and smell, some writers have identified what they believe is a further sense, that of balance and equilibrium, governed by the vestibular system in the body. *(For some accounts of this, see* Leaves Before the Wind *and* Rapport, *issue 18.)* NLP works with each of the senses and helps people to make distinctions between how they perceive the detail of each of them.

The Sense of Sight

As well as actually seeing things, you can imagine them in your mind, ie mentally visualize them. The mental sub-modalities of sight include:

★ distance (Are you imagining things close to yourself or far away?)
★ brightness (Do you have a bright image or a dull one?)
★ colour (Do you have a black-and-white picture in your mind or a coloured one?)
★ movement (Do you see pictures as if they were photographs or as if they were movie films?)
★ size (Do you imagine large or small images?)
★ self-perception (Do you see yourself in your images or not?)

The Sense of Hearing

Part of hearing is sensing external sounds and part is imagining sounds, including that of your own voice, in your head.

Sub-modalities of sound can include:

★ volume (Is a sound loud or quiet?)
★ pitch (Does a sound have a high or low pitch?)
★ speed (Is a sound – such as a person's voice – fast or slow?)
★ tonality (Is the tone pleasant or unpleasant?)
★ proximity (Is a sound coming from close by or far off?)

The Sense of Touch

Sub-modalities of touch can include:

★ warmth (Warm or cool?)
★ texture (Rough or smooth?)
★ density (Heavy or light?)

Also included in this category is non-tactile feeling (ie emotional responses) including, for example, calmness, enthusiasm, sadness and energy.

The Sense of Taste
Sub-modalities of taste include:

★ sweetness
★ sourness
★ bitterness

The Sense of Smell
Sub-modalities of smell include:

★ acridity
★ sweetness
★ freshness

So each of the senses has its sub-divisions and a major feature of NLP is its ability to help people make fine distinctions between elements and then manipulate these elements in their imagination to create new and effective experiences, to consider the impact of future events, to review past occurrences and to become more motivated to bring about change.

Because of the power of the mind, sub-modality changes can bring about major shifts in thinking and feeling, with resultant effects in behavioural terms, and I will be exploring this further in Section Two of this book.

Rapport
Another area for which NLP is well known is helping people create and maintain good relationships. Developing rapport is a vital first step to relating to others effectively and there are some very specific NLP techniques for achieving this, which I will be discussing in Chapter 5.

Future Pacing/New Behaviour Generation

'Future pacing' is the process whereby a person imagines doing something in the future in order to check what the results might be. It is an invaluable aid to decision-making. One particular application of future pacing is the New Behaviour Generator developed by Leslie Cameron Bandler, which uses a combination of role modelling and future pacing to first imagine a new way of acting and then mentally experience it. *(See Chapters 4 and 6 for more on these techniques.)*

Swish/Fast Phobia Cures and Perspective Patterns

These techniques use changes in how the mind perceives reality and offer rapid ways of helping people change their perception of situations. Although obvious precursors exist, the swish pattern has been attributed to Richard Bandler and the fast phobia cure to Bandler and Grinder, and perspective patterns were developed by John McWhirter.

Swish and perspective pattern techniques may use various senses and there is also a similarity to DHE *(see 'Developments in NLP' page 84)*. For example, a positive mental image may be superimposed on a negative one in order to reprogramme the mind to respond in a positive way to a situation. Alternatively, positive sounds or dialogue may be substituted for negative ones, or compared to negative ones, in order to put them in perspective. The actual techniques for doing this can vary according to the process used.

Approaches to phobias include helping people to experience situations in a detached way, bringing some novelty to a situation by using humour or exaggeration, or altering perception of time so that it is experienced as speeded up, slowed down or reversed.

I do not believe it is appropriate to go into further detail on these techniques here, as they offer very powerful ways of working with difficult or traumatic events and need to be used under supervision. If you wish to explore them further, you can locate a trained practitioner or therapist through the details given in the Appendix.

Developments in NLP

As NLP has progressed, there have been many new and associated developments. New Code NLP, mentioned above, was one of the major developments in the earlier days. Another development has been Design Human Engineering (DHE), created by Richard Bandler. This includes elements such as imaginary control panels to help people alter their personal experiences – particularly useful in pain control and the enhancement of motivation – and the use of external sounds (often music or speech) to remove negative self-criticism by substituting it with more positive mental patterns. With these approaches, the ways in which new patterns are installed is important to their success.

Other developments include Tad James' Time Line Therapy, a way of taking a person back in time, in a trance state, to identify and neutralize emotional traumas; Judith DeLozier's Somatic Syntax, using the fact that body movements have structure, rather like sentences, and utilizing this awareness to enhance actions and interactions; John McWhirter's Developmental Behavioural Modelling (DBM), a systematic approach using fractal modelling to create and apply models in all levels of human experience; and Francine Shapiro's Eye Movement Desensitization Reprocessing (EMDR), therapeutic handling of unprocessed blockages and traumas through guided eye movements, which is not strict NLP, but utilizes similar premises. Connirae and Steve Andreas developed a similar NLP process – Eye Movement Integrator – at about the same time.

This chapter has covered some of the better-known NLP approaches and techniques. Frameworks and models are not complete explanations of reality, but are helpful guides to how people function. Techniques cannot be used in isolation; they may be helpful, but need to be set in the context of the whole person and the whole situation. The next section of the book goes on to explore how some of the techniques I have been discussing can be applied in your everyday life.

Section Two

This part of the book contains the practical elements of NLP; how you can use its techniques and approaches in your own life to enhance your achievement.

The chapters which follow are divided into contextual areas. Chapter 4 covers personal growth, Chapter 5 covers relationships and Chapter 6 covers work and business. In order to give a shape to the applications chapters, certain techniques have been selected to illustrate how you can apply NLP in your own daily activities. It is worth remembering, however, that this division is somewhat arbitrary, as NLP techniques are all useful across a wide range of contexts.

Chapter 4

Personal Growth

We all change throughout life; this is an inevitable process. Without change we would stagnate and fail to keep up with the world around us. Growth, however, is another thing altogether. People have different definitions of growth, but as a working premise, we can take the idea that it involves reaching different levels of thinking, feeling, behaving or being. So growth is different from change in that it is beyond what currently exists, rather than simply different.

If you think about the various areas of your life, you can consider to what extent you are achieving the levels of development, or success, you desire. It may be that, in some areas, you do not know what you would like to attain, or it may be that there are areas which are, at present, something of a blank book – you may not even know of their existence, or it may be that you know what you would like to achieve, but do not know how to bring about the changes which are required.

In this chapter we will take some areas of personal growth and consider how NLP can help you attain a higher stage of development. We will also explore in more depth some of the techniques covered in Chapter 3 and apply them in the following areas:

- ★ self-esteem, resourcefulness and emotional control (what happens in your mind)
- ★ health and fitness (what happens in your body)
- ★ learning and skills development (what happens in your performance)
- ★ spirituality (what happens in your awareness)

Processes

Before embarking on this exploration, there are two processes which are useful to consider: self-awareness and movement. Let's consider each of these briefly.

Self-awareness

In order to make the most of the techniques discussed (and, in a broader context, to make the most of opportunities life presents to you), it helps if you have a reasonable degree of self-awareness. Self-awareness usually entails a recognition of what you are able to do, what you actually do, how you do it and the results of having done it; this includes your behaviour, your thoughts, your feelings and your beliefs, values and assumptions *(as outlined in Chapter 1)*.

Movement

Movement includes the process of change and progress. It is impossible to stand still in life, but knowing where you want to get to and how to get there is not always easy. NLP has a process that helps with this concept of movement; it has three elements, as follows:

★ **Present state:** The situation which currently exists in relation to an issue. For example, if you do not yet know how to rollerskate, your current state is one of *lack of experience.*

★ **Desired state:** What you want to achieve in relation to this issue. So, keeping the rollerskating example, the desired state might be one of *competent performance.*

★ **The steps to take (or transition from present state to desired state):** To make the change, it is necessary to take some action and so, keeping the same example, you might have lessons in rollerskating.

So, the two processes which inform the whole of this chapter, and also the two further applications chapters which follow, are self-awareness and movement. By understanding yourself, knowing where you are currently, what you would like to achieve and how to get there, you have the foundation for achieving success.

The remainder of this chapter covers some common situations where you might wish to make changes in your life and gives suggestions as to how they might be tackled, using NLP. Each example involves using the process outlined above; ie identifying present situation, desired situation and the steps to take, with the steps to take including an appropriate NLP technique. If any of the examples given do not apply to you, simply transfer the techniques to comparable situations of your own. The categories covered are as outlined above, ie self-esteem and resourcefulness, health and fitness, learning and skills development, spirituality.

Self-esteem, Resourcefulness and Emotional Control

Most of us have times when we feel self-assured and resourceful and times when we feel disempowered. Sometimes we may put the latter down to external forces, saying things like 'They made me feel really bad', 'It gave me a problem' or 'I was a victim of circumstances.'

In practice, however, we are all ultimately responsible for our own thoughts, feelings, responses and behaviour and, however difficult or restricting circumstances may be, we have facilities for overcoming obstacles and problems. Of course, doing this may not always be easy and we may not always know exactly how to tackle difficult situations, but if we adopt a positive and practical approach, many things can be improved.

So what can NLP offer in this area? The most useful NLP techniques here are to do with mental processing; in other words, using your mind to make changes in your perception and in your creativity. Let us take some imaginary people and see how NLP could assist them in particular situations.

Self-esteem

Self-esteem can manifest itself across a wide range of situations, so that a person may feel high or low self-esteem generally. The following example is simply one illustration of where self-esteem could be enhanced.

Present Situation

Cathy feels her opinions have little value and that nobody would want to listen to them and she also believes that other people generally know more than she does and are more competent than she is. She tries hard to please her friends and family, but feels that whatever she does is not good enough. She finds it hard to think of herself as a success.

Desired Situation

Because Cathy's self-esteem is low, she finds it difficult to even think of things being different, but, if pressed, will admit that it would be nice if, when meeting new people, she felt she had something worthwhile and interesting to say to them. She also wishes to believe that when she does something, such as cooking a meal or organizing an event, that she is capable of doing it well.

Steps to Take

Cathy could use 'internal dialogue' to improve the way she thinks about herself. Internal dialogue relates to the 'inner voices' many of us have in our heads, telling us things about what we are doing and how others are responding to us. Sometimes these inner voices may be our own voice; sometimes they may be voices of people we know; often they are negative and critical. (Inner voices are not, of course, 'real' sounds, only imagined ones.)

Cathy may, at present, imagine herself saying things like 'I'm not very good at things', 'I can't do things right', 'What I think isn't important.' She may imagine other people saying negative things about her such as 'Cathy isn't very interesting' or 'She didn't do that very well.'

With such negative dialogue going on, it isn't surprising if Cathy believes herself to be inferior to others.

With NLP, Cathy could change her internal dialogue so that she thinks to herself: 'I *am* capable at the things I do', 'I *can* find some interesting things to say to this person', 'I *am* as valuable as other people.' She could also let any imagined criticisms from other people become less audible in her head and substitute more positive thoughts; she could imagine people saying they have enjoyed talking to her and complimenting her on things she has done.

This goes beyond just 'positive thinking'; as it is important to *actually imagine hearing the positive words in your head*, as if they are really happening. Because your mind does not differentiate between fact and fiction (imagine a lemon slice in your mouth and notice if your mouth waters even though the lemon is not real), you can put these new voices into your imagination and your mind will accept them as if they were real. In this way it is possible to have a new perception of reality and a more positive self-concept.

Resourcefulness: Confidence

Resourcefulness can be similar to self-esteem in that it can also cross contexts, but in most cases people wish to feel resourceful in a particular situation, such as feeling confident, being motivated, feeling enthusiastic, being persistent about *something in particular*. One very specific element of resourcefulness is being able to maintain a sense of humour when faced with difficult circumstances.

Here are some examples of how it is possible to generate personal feelings of resourcefulness using NLP.

Present Situation

James has to give a speech at his daughter's wedding. He has never liked speaking in public and thinks he will sound dull, look ill at ease and feel anxious. He doesn't think he can project his voice well and believes that he will be unable to remember what to say. He doesn't have a perception of himself as a natural, witty speaker.

Desired Situation

James would like to be able to stand up confidently, sound interesting and amusing and look as if he is enjoying the speech. He wants to be able to control his nerves and remember what to say.

Steps to Take

James is used to the way he has felt in the past on similar occasions – awkward and ill at ease. What happens when you feel this way is that your body gets into the posture it remembers from past uncomfortable experiences.

James also, however, has past experiences of feeling much more confident and at ease. At these times he is able to move freely, breathe easily and look at people in a friendly and welcoming way.

To feel better at the wedding, James needs to re-access such feelings and, by doing so, re-access the posture, movement and gestures which accompany the feelings. NLP can help him do this.

What James needs to do is remember a specific time when he felt very confident. He can access this time by remembering: What could he see? What did the place look like? Was he inside or outside? What colours and shapes could he see? What scenery or furnishings? What could he hear? Were there people talking? Was there music playing or was it very quiet and peaceful? Was he feeling any physical sensations? Was he warm or cool? Was he standing or sitting? Was he holding or touching anything? Did he have a taste in his mouth from eating or drinking? Was there a scent in the air? Finally he can remember the feeling of confidence and relaxation and notice where in his body this is (for example, his head, stomach, chest or all over).

Once James has gone through this process, he will have reminded himself that he can feel confident and what it is physically like to do so. Once he has recalled this, his body will begin to take up a similar stance to the one it had on the past occasion when he felt confident – his posture will shift, his breathing will shift, his expression will change.

Now all he has to do is to capture this physiological change in his memory. When he has to make the speech, he can adopt this posture, breathing pattern, expression and movement and he will then look and sound confident and feel much more able to carry out the task in a competent manner, and one that is enjoyable for both him and his audience.

Resourcefulness: Patience

Present Situation

Peter's mother is elderly and has developed Alzheimer's disease. She forgets what she has said and keeps repeating things; she wanders out of the house and has to be tracked down; she puts the kettle on a hotplate on the cooker and boils it dry; she wakes Peter up in the night by wandering around and knocking things over. Peter is very stressed by having to deal with this situation and finds himself getting frustrated, tired and snappy.

Desired Situation

Peter knows his mother can't help what she does and he would like to be able to see the funny side of things rather than getting angry. He would also like to be able to cope with having less sleep than he needs.

Steps to Take

Peter has become very weighed down by the situation he is in. Although it is serious, it would help if he could see a lighter side to it. What he can do is use the NLP anchoring technique to help himself inject a little (appropriate) humour into what is happening.

'Anchoring' simply means making an association between a situation and a trigger so that when the trigger is activated, the response to the situation can be changed. Peter probably already has many negative anchors (triggers) for the present situation. For example, his mother's voice may act as a trigger to make him feel irritated or the sight of the kettle she boils dry could be a trigger for him feeling anxious.

It would not be appropriate for Peter to disregard his feelings; however, it would be better for him to have more resourceful feelings than irritation and anxiety. NLP can help Peter to harness humour as an alternative way of responding.

What Peter could do is to think of a time when he found a situation amusing. He could think himself back into this situation just as James did in the previous example about public speaking. Once Peter really remembers the amusing situation he can give himself a trigger (perhaps biting the end of his tongue very gently), so that this trigger is associated with the feeling of amusement. A few practice runs will associate the trigger with the memory.

Now, when Peter hears his mother's voice or sees the kettle he can *bite his tongue!* This will generate the feeling of amusement, leaving Peter to decide whether he actually needs to do more about the situation or whether he can just allow it to wash over him in a calm way.

Anchoring is a powerful technique and one which can be really helpful in becoming more positive and resourceful.

Emotional Control

Many people have had experiences that have had a major impact on them. Often these experiences are very positive and life-enhancing, but sometimes they result in overwhelming feelings such as anger, grief, resentment and fear. Sometimes these feelings persist, or resurface over a period of time.

The NLP approach to trauma is generally forward, not backward, looking. In other words, it does not work by getting the person to relive a past experience in order to exorcise it, nor does it work by exploring the reasons for a memory persisting (ie an analytical approach based on the content of the memory). NLP usually works through helping a person elicit their 'desired state' – what they would like instead – and then finding ways of assisting them to access that alternative way of being.

I will not give a 'case study' example here, but will just explain some circumstances in which you might work on this area. Some 'desired states' might be acceptance rather than anger, appreciation rather then grief, tolerance rather than resentment and calmness instead of fear. To achieve such states, a technique that is often used by therapists involves 'viewing' the traumatic event in a detached way, so that it is possible to experience it as an 'observer' rather than relive it as a participant. By detaching yourself in this way, the feelings associated with an event become distanced and it is possible to review what has happened and respond to it in a more appropriate manner.

If you wish to work on a personal issue of this nature, an NLP psychotherapist will be able to help you *(see Useful Addresses for details of how to find a psychotherapist).*

Health and Fitness

People nowadays are much more aware of the benefits that come from good health and a high degree of personal fitness. While not everyone wishes to be a top sportsperson, there are many elements of physical health and fitness that can be achieved by the average person.

The following examples are to do with making changes in how your mind represents reality and making links between perception and responses:

Weight Control
Present Situation
Liz is rather overweight. Her hair is often dull and looks lifeless. She doesn't have as much energy as she would like.

Desired Situation

Liz thinks her weight is affecting her health, as it stops her from being as active as she would like. She would also like to look better; while not wishing to become waif-like, she would like to be able to fit into average-sized clothes.

Steps to Take

Because Liz believes she is overweight, when she looks in her mirror she sees her present self looking back out and her mind only has this image to work with.

It seems that our minds are best motivated when they have a real goal to work towards, and when this goal is represented in a visual way. For Liz to change, she needs to believe that she can be the way she wants.

What Liz can do is write down her goal as if she had already achieved it and then picture it as if it were real. So, she might write down: 'I weigh nine stone. I can get into a size 14 dress and my hair and skin look good.' She should then make a mental image of the new Liz. This image should be as motivating as possible, which means it will probably be bright, colourful and close up, with movement and activity.

Once Liz's mind has seen this picture, and continues seeing it, she is likely to be more motivated to achieve her result – she really is 'keeping it in mind'. NLP suggests that each person has an optimum way of visualizing particular things; for example picturing them at a certain distance, a certain angle, a certain size and so forth. With help, Liz could find out her own best way of doing this and really make progress towards her goal. She still has to do the work of eating sensibly and exercising appropriately if she is to lose weight, but the mental image will keep her focused and motivated to do this.

Alleviating Allergies

Many people occasionally have medical complaints that are slow to clear. Using NLP techniques, sometimes in conjunction with hypnosis, can provide ways of alleviating symptoms and combating illness, although it is important to emphasize that NLP, or other non-medical techniques, should not be used as a substitute for professional medical help where this is the most appropriate approach to a condition.

Let's take allergies as an example. If you have had an allergic reaction to something, it may well have been diagnosed medically and treated with drugs. If this has worked, that's fine. If, however, medication has not produced the result you need, or if you wish to explore other means of alleviation, you may be interested in a technique that appears to work well for some people (Dilts, Smith and Hallbom, *Beliefs*, Metamorphous Press, 1990).

This technique is based on the concept that an allergy is simply a mistake that has been made by the immune system, whereby something that is basically harmless causes the body to respond in an inappropriate way. You will need a trained practitioner to guide you through the technique, which involves finding something that is comparable to the thing that triggers the allergic response but to which you have no allergic response. You would then be helped to imagine yourself with this non-threatening thing, build up a positive response to it and then transfer that positive response to the original thing to which your body reacted by producing the allergic response.

The NLP approach to allergies is just one example of how people can be helped to respond in different ways to medical conditions, both physical and mental. Some other areas in which good results have been claimed for NLP include arthritis, poor eyesight, tinnitus, pain control (including pain experienced in chronic complaints and terminal illnesses), anxiety, depression, phobias and eating disorders.

With medical conditions, in addition to the techniques already described, the NLP approaches used may include the following:

★ reframing – experiencing a condition from a different perspective, such as considering a broken leg as providing an opportunity to catch up on reading; sometimes there are hidden benefits in ill-nesses which a different way of thinking can reveal, and sometimes viewing an illness in a new light can help alleviate symptoms

★ sub-modality work – making changes in how your mind represents the situation, for example picturing yourself as fit and healthy or hearing your voice saying you are improving on a daily basis

★ programming for control – for example imagining pain levels as points on a dial and then moving to a new position on the dial in order to lessen the pain experienced

★ shifting beliefs – for example believing you are capable of seeing without glasses

★ using hypnotic trance states – for example to speed up the healing process after an operation through suggestion techniques, a process that is increasingly being used in conventional surgery

★ vizualization – for example imagining cancer cells as snowballs being melted by the heat of the body's immune system

★ 'parts' work – identifying 'parts' of a person which are responsible for creating symptoms and then identifying more creative parts that can produce more desirable results

★ analysis of behaviour patterns – analysing what a person does and substituting other activities that are likely to produce greater benefits

If you are interested in finding out more about such approaches to medical conditions, NLP therapists will be able to help you *(see Useful Addresses for how to contact a therapist).*

Motivation to Exercise
Present Situation

Jenny gets out of breath running for a bus, tends to lack energy by early afternoon and thinks her muscle tone is rather soft. She does go to the gym to keep fit, but finds it difficult to maintain interest when she is using the equipment, getting rather bored with long periods spent jogging or stepping.

Desired Situation

Jenny would like to be able to maintain her motivation while working out, especially while using equipment which takes up quite a bit of time.

Steps to Take

While at the gym, Jenny is very conscious of the unchanging surroundings. If she were in a place which was more stimulating to all her senses, she would probably find time passing faster. So what Jenny can do is imagine she is somewhere else.

To do this, she could think of a real place she knows, which she enjoys visiting. This may be a distant location or may be close to home, perhaps even somewhere as simple as the local shops.

Now all Jenny has to do is imagine, while she is on her jogger at the gym, is that she is really taking a walk to the shops. She should imagine doing the walk in real time – feeling her feet stepping on the ground, seeing the sights she would actually pass on the real walk, hearing any sounds which there might be in that environment, feeling the temperature and smelling any scents in the air.

As Jenny goes on her imaginary walk, her mind becomes more stimulated, her conscious awareness of her real surroundings diminishes and her thoughts become more self-absorbed and imaginative. In much less time than usual she will have completed her exercise and also had the mental stimulation of the imaginary walk.

Next time she can choose a different walk or even a different context, such as an imaginary discussion with a friend, working on a problem which needs to be solved or planning a future event. All these processes, when made real enough, will act to distort time and make an activity seem to pass more quickly.

Jenny still needs to pay conscious attention to her exercise technique, but with practice, she can do this as well as allowing her mind to relax when it is not needed for conscious activity.

Sports Performance

A good deal has been written about enhancing sports performance through mental as well as physical processes, and there are books on specific sports as well as general guides to improvement. In this section we will cover just one element – the use of mental practice to enhance skills.

It has been found that mental practice is extremely effective in developing skills. With real-life practice, some moves will be done excellently, but others less well. With mental practice, however, it is possible to repeat, in your mind, time after time, a move that you remember doing in the past. If the original move was really good, the imagined ones will be just as good. It seems that this repeated imagined activity stimulates nerve connections in the brain in the same way that real activities do. This sets up pathways for repeated excellence and, because there will be no errors in your mental activity, the repeated movements will enhance the skill when put into practice in real life – often more so than real-life practice.

As an example of this, if you take the sport of fencing and wish to be able to improve a particular move, you can imagine the various elements of that move as you have done it in the past. For example, some of the things you can imagine are the weight and shape of the sword's handle in your hand, the direction and speed of your arm as you execute the move, the sound of the blade as it meets that of your opponent, the rhythm and pace of the movement as it takes place. By reliving this experience, you can mentally rehearse the move, adding any aspects that will refine and improve it. When you come to do the move for real, the mental practice will have helped your development of the skill.

Learning and Skills Development

We all learn and develop as we go through life, sometimes deliberately, at other times in an unplanned way. Learning encompasses knowledge, understanding and skills development and all of these help us enhance our performance of the various activities in which we are engaged. NLP can help with your efforts at self-improvement.

In the following examples, we are again considering ways of changing mental responses.

Spelling
Present State
Tom thinks he isn't good at spelling. He has been assessed for dyslexia and that isn't the problem; he just finds it difficult to remember how words are composed.

Desired State
Tom would like to be able to spell words easily, especially when he makes job applications and wants to put things in a way which will reflect well on him.

Steps to Take

NLP has a strategy for spelling, developed largely by Robert Dilts, with other members of the original group at Santa Cruz *(see Chapter 2)* also being involved. In fact, it was this work on the spelling strategy that started off the broader work on strategies that has become a major foundation of NLP. The American Sid Jacobson does a good deal of work in this area and is renowned for the rapid changes he can bring about in people with long-established problems with reading. He has popularized the spelling strategy in his book *Meta-cation*.

Research indicates that people who spell well have one particular thing in common: they are good at picturing things and visualize the word they wish to spell as they think about it. Tom, therefore, needs to embark on a programme of developing his visual sense. When he comes across a word he needs to spell, he should first get himself into a positive state (the anchoring techniques mentioned earlier will help with this) and then he can look at the word in print, close his eyes and picture it on the page. It will almost certainly help if he moves his eyes upwards as he does this, as this helps to activate the part of the brain which produces images. As Tom practises this skill, he will find it easier to 'see' the word, and when this happens, he will find he can spell it both backwards and forwards, if he chooses.

Studying and Taking Examinations

Present State

Kelly finds it hard to concentrate at school. Somehow, although she tries to pay attention, she doesn't seem to be able to concentrate on what her teacher is saying.

Desired State

Kelly wants to do well at school so she can go on to train as a physiotherapist, but doesn't know how she is going to pass her exams unless she takes in more of her schoolwork. She wants to find her lessons interesting and remember what she is told. She wants to know that she will be able to enjoy taking her exams and showing what she can do.

Steps to Take

Accelerated learning has contributed to NLP an awareness that people have individual ways of learning. These may include picturing things, hearing things, using logic, using numbers, doing physical movements, working with others, working alone and so forth. In particular, NLP has shown how the use of all five senses (sight, sound, touch, taste and smell) can enhance a learning process. Kelly has found her lessons hard to keep up with because she is not very 'auditory' (good at using her sense of hearing and manipulation of words) and her teacher, not knowing about accelerated learning, has relied mainly upon *telling* her students things, *reading to them*, and getting them to *read books*. Kelly learns much better when she is *shown* things and can *get a feel* for what they are and how they work.

Kelly can take a number of steps to help herself learn. The first of these is to do with using her visual sense. First she can draw herself 'mind maps' (a concept developed by Tony Buzan and illustrated in books such as *The Mind Map Book*) to give herself a good picture of each topic and how its different elements interrelate. A mind map is a diagram using words, pictures, colours and interconnecting lines to put a topic together as a visual image, as the illustration shows.

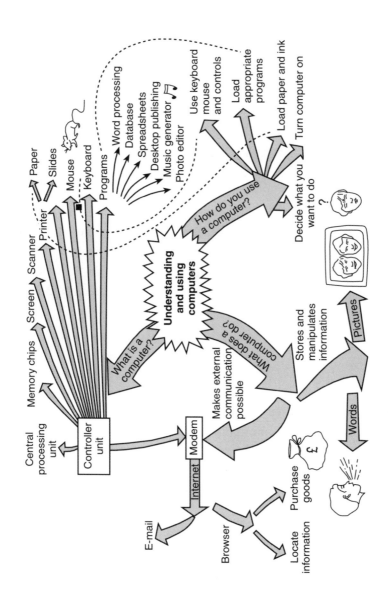

A mind map about understanding and using computers

There is good evidence that effective students naturally use the mind-mapping process, even if they have not been shown it by someone else. Cricket Kemp explored this with pupils in colleges in England to excellent effect. Kelly will benefit from using such techniques and thus being able to see things for herself, rather than just hearing them said by her teacher.

The second thing Kelly can do is to help herself 'get a feel for' the subjects she is studying, to make them more tangible. She could do this in different ways; one possibility would be to get some 'hands-on' experience of the topics. So, for example, in her biology class, after seeing pictures of how joints work and looking at animals, Kelly could feel her own joints to see how the principles work in real people. By doing this she will be bringing the lessons to life and giving herself the bodily experience she has lacked in the lessons.

There are many books on accelerated learning techniques *(see Bibliography)*.

Spirituality

Awareness of Higher Levels

Personal growth is not only about developments in knowledge and skills, it is also about the relationship between tangible, existential elements of life and those elements which cannot be quantified and physically handled but bring an awareness of forces beyond our conscious existence.

Many people work in the area of NLP and spirituality, Robert Dilts being one notable example, and there are ways of using NLP in order to access personal understanding and development of spiritual awareness. Do note that, in NLP, spirituality is not about religion or religious belief, although it could be for any particular individual.

The following examples use modelling as a process for expanding awareness.

Present Situation

Mark has spent his life working in a very practical way, as an engineer. He has recently become involved with a new partner, who attends religious services each week. He is beginning to feel a little left out at times.

Desired Situation

Mark does not feel any inclination towards organized religion, but has become curious about his partner's beliefs and would like to explore the possibility of what lies beyond his everyday life.

Steps to Take

Mark could adopt the NLP process of 'modelling' (copying) people who have some belief in 'what is beyond'. To do this he could:

★ read about the different kinds of belief people have
★ research what people do in order to extend their spiritual awareness – meditation, observation of patterns in nature and so forth
★ do exercises designed to bring about shifts in perception, for example imagining taking on the perspective of a higher being, or his own 'higher self', by imagining how such a 'higher entity' might perceive people and how they go about their lives (thanks to Penny Tompkins and James Lawley for these exercises)
★ find his 'core values' by identifying things he really wants and what he would gain if he had them. To do this he could ask himself questions such as: 'What is the most important thing to me about ... and if I had that, what...?' *(See* Core Transformation *by Connirae Andreas, Real People, Press, 1979, for more on this topic.)* He could also represent these core values by a symbol or metaphor.

★ find a symbol or metaphor for his purpose, sense of direction or mission in life, or for a connection with something greater than himself – for example thinking of his purpose as if it were a beacon shining brightly, thinking of his sense of direction as an upward spiral or thinking of his connection with an entity beyond himself as a magnetic field

Sense of Purpose
Present Situation
Helen feels she is lacking a sense of purpose in her life. She is very occupied with day-to-day affairs, but is not sure what they are leading to.

Desired State
She would like to know what it is that she contributes and whether it is part of any greater whole beyond herself.

Steps to Take
Helen can think of a number of times when she is really 'being herself', times when she feels fulfilled and happy. She can then tell another person about these times or, if she prefers to keep their content private, write down the details. She can then find a few key words, phrases or events which seem to keep cropping up. For example, she might find that these times are about 'helping others', 'bringing about change' and 'having fun'. Helen can then, with her friend's help if necessary, find a phrase which sums up her personal mission via these words, for example: 'I help people create things they want in a lighthearted way.'

By using her own experience as a basis for finding a common thread, Helen is becoming more aware of a personal mission which can go beyond her normal everyday existence. Making such connections is one approach to gaining some spiritual awareness. (This example is based on one of the steps in David Gordon's 'Meaningful Existence' model.)

Before leaving this chapter, I would like to say more about a technique which is basic to NLP and which underlies many efforts at self-development. The technique is role modelling, generally shortened to just 'modelling' in NLP terminology, which has been referred to earlier in this book.

Modelling involves finding a person who does something in a way you would like to emulate and then copying what they do in order to achieve similar results. As we saw in Chapter 1, this is the process which really started off NLP – the attempt to observe, and quantify, then transfer to others, the elements of effective performance from outstanding people. Many of the examples I have given in this chapter focus on modelling, either other people or yourself.

In any area where you would like to improve or develop, it is well worth finding yourself a role model to emulate. Role modelling, by the way, does not mean 'becoming' the same person as the role model, it simply means utilizing a part of that person's behaviour in a way which is appropriate for you. This is how we all learn; from our earliest days we copy those around us in order to try out different behaviour. NLP just suggests we continue this into adult life and make a practice of learning from others.

There is one particular NLP technique which uses this role-modelling process in a very simple way; it is the New Behaviour Generator, mentioned earlier, developed by Judith DeLozier. This process allows you to try out new behaviour in your mind before using it in real life, which gives you an opportunity to review the behaviour and check whether it would, in fact, be appropriate for you to copy.

The process involves visualizing and so you may wish to practise some basic visualization techniques before beginning:

★ Look at an illustration in a book. Describe to yourself (out loud or in your head) whatever you can see. Close your eyes and remember as much of the illustration as you can, including the colours, the shapes, the proximity of one part of the illustration to another and so on.

★ Look at yourself in a mirror. Again, say what you see in as much detail as possible. Close your eyes and recall that detail (the colour of your eyes, the shape of your mouth, the length of your hair, and so on).

★ Think about a place you visited some time ago. Keep your eyes open and remember as much as you can about how the place looked (scenery, buildings, decorations, colours, shapes and so on). Close your eyes and notice if it is easier to remember those same elements.

★ Close your eyes and imagine seeing the following: a bicycle, an apple, a teapot, an elephant, a beach, clouds in the sky.

★ Close your eyes and imagine seeing the following: a giant ant, a tiny aeroplane, a soft table, a hard blade of grass, a green pigeon, a blue banana, a camera with hands, a transparent person.

Now you have done these exercises, have a go at the New Behaviour Generator:

1. Find a quiet place and sit or lie in a comfortable position.
2. Think of something you would like to be able to do, or something you already do which you would like to do better.
3. Think of a person (your role model) whom you have observed doing that thing. This may be a person you know yourself or it may be someone you have seen on television.
4. In your mind, make an image of the person doing that behaviour and watch it as clearly as you can. See how the person sits, stands or moves; watch their gestures and the expression on their face; imagine the sound of their voice; notice how other people are reacting to them. Once you have done this, check that you would like to be able to do this yourself.
5. In your mind, substitute yourself for the other person and, as if you were distanced from yourself, watch yourself behaving in the same

way. Remember, this is not about being the other person, simply copying one element of their behaviour. Again, check that you would still like to do things in that way.

6. Now, imagine 'stepping into' your mental image and feeling what it would be like to behave in that way. Notice how your body feels when you behave like that; notice the sound of your voice if you are speaking; notice how any other people around seem to respond to you. Really become aware of what it is like to behave like that now. Again, check that that behaviour is consistent with who you are.

7. Think of a situation in the near future when it would be desirable and appropriate to use that behaviour. In your mind, make a mental image of behaving in that way. If you are happy with that, move on to the next step.

8. Again, imagine stepping into that experience and really feel what it is like to behave like that in the real situation. Enjoy the experience of your new skill.

Doing this exercise gives your mind the sense that you have already behaved like that in reality; when you come to do it for real, it will be easier and more enjoyable.

Last Points

This chapter has presented some of the techniques and approaches that distinguish NLP's contribution to the development of personal excellence. The approaches and techniques discussed can be used to encourage imagination and problem solving at both conscious and unconscious levels and can contribute to both personal development and healing.

NLP takes a holistic view of change work, so that shifts in one element, such as behaviour, thoughts, feelings or beliefs, impinge on others in a systemic way. This means that whenever a change process is undertaken, its impact on the individual as a whole needs to be taken into account.

Scientific research is proving the links between mind and body which until recently have been the subject of debate, with evidence accumulating on the importance of positive mental and emotional states on physical health and personal achievement. NLP has much to offer in the field of personal enhancement.

Chapter 5

Social Relationships

Having considered personal growth, we can now move on to ways of enhancing interactions with others and this chapter will give you a range of ways to create and maintain good relationships.

There are many occasions when we need to come into contact with other people. These include social events with friends or colleagues, family events, dealings with neighbours, using professional services (doctors, electricians, accountants, car mechanics and so forth) and dealing with educational services for ourselves or our children. The list is lengthy and varied.

Each of the relationships mentioned above has its own characteristics but there are common threads running through them all. In each case, the interaction is enhanced if an effective relationship can be created quickly and maintained as long as required. NLP offers ways of doing just this – developing good and lasting relationships with other people.

Personal communications play a major part in dealing with other people and there are a range of ways in which you can communicate. Communication involves both *what* you say (the content) and *the way in which you say it* (the process). You can communicate verbally, through words, or non-verbally, through ways which do not involve spoken or written language – for example appearance, gesture, posture and movement. Your voice tone can also communicate things; although this does involve speech, it is usually classified as 'non-verbal communication' as it does not depend on the actual words being spoken, but rather the *way* in which they are spoken.

Interaction may be on a one-to one basis or between several people; it may be face to face or on the telephone, through the internet or via written communications, such as letters or faxes. On the whole, the term 'social relationships' implies face-to-face contact, but establishing relationships in some of the other ways listed above is also important and requires equivalent skills.

If you have ever felt at a loss as to how to deal with others, if you have felt anxious about meeting people or making small talk, if you have been concerned about dealing with those in authority, if you have worried about doing something embarrassing when in company, if you have found it difficult to assert yourself, or if you have wondered how to handle conflict with, or between, others, or if you have found it difficult to control your feelings or express yourself fluently, then this section can help you.

There are a number of steps involved in dealing with others; these include having an objective, planning what to do or say, managing how you feel, using observation and listening skills, communicating effectively, gaining rapport and influencing. It is also vital to be flexible and to monitor and review what you do, so that you can assess how effective it has been and whether to do something similar again in the future. I will be covering some of these topics in Chapter 6, on work and business applications, so will concentrate here on the basic steps which are involved in person-to-person contact. These steps are:

★ using observation skills
★ shifting perspective

★ creating and maintaining rapport
★ using language flexibly
★ being persuasive and influential

Using Observation Skills

Noticing how other people are behaving and reacting is a very useful skill. It is surprising how often people 'mind read' others' behaviour and say things like 'She looked very bored', 'He was clearly confused' or 'They sounded rather aloof.' All these observations could have been correct, but equally could have been a misinterpretation of someone else's behaviour. For example, yawning *could* indicate boredom, but could just as easily indicate tiredness or lack of oxygen.

To ensure you understand another person, it is useful to treat their behaviour simply as information, without evaluating it, and then to check what they are really feeling or thinking. It is possible to do this directly by asking them about their thoughts or feelings and it is also possible to check indirectly by testing out your own observations and looking for other evidence to support your interpretation.

The NLP term for observation is 'sensory acuity' – using your senses to pick up signals. If you would like to become more skilled at observation, have a go at the following activities.

★ Watch people on public transport. Notice how they look just before they reach the stop where they get off. Begin to notice how their behaviour changes at this stage – for example, where they look, whether they shift position, when they reach for any things they have put on the floor. Watching in this way will help you become aware of the early signs of reactions to circumstances. It may even get you a seat too!

★ Ask a person you know if they will help with an exercise. If they agree, ask them to sit in a chair and then to think of a person they like. As they think of this person, notice their posture in the chair, any movement they are making with their hands or feet, their head position, their eye movements, whether their mouth changes (eg widens or turns up), where their eyes are focusing (in the distance or close up) and the direction in which they are looking. Then ask them to think of a person they do not like and notice the same elements, this time also looking for differences between their appearance when thinking about the first person and when thinking about the second person. Finally, ask the person to think of either the person they like or the person they dislike and guess which of the two it is. Repeat the process until you are correct each time and then have a go at doing it with someone else.

★ Watch and listen to a person you are with frequently. Become aware of exactly how they look and sound when in different states. For example, what tone of voice goes with pleasure or irritation, what posture goes with energy or lethargy, what eye movements go with past memories or future expectations.

Doing these exercises will help you hone your observation skills and become more sensitive and responsive to other people's experiences. By enhancing your understanding of, and responsiveness towards, others, you are likely to find that your relationships with them improve and misunderstandings become easier to avoid.

Shifting Perspective

The NLP term for shifting perspectives is 'taking on different perceptual positions'. In everyday language, people often use phrases which refer to positions, such as 'If I were in your position I would do things differently.' This kind of statement recognizes the fact that people do differ in how they act and that we can imagine being in someone else's 'position'. (Although a speaker I heard on the radio some years ago said, 'Although we may say, "If I were in your position, I would do this," what we actually mean is: "If you were in my position, you would do this"!')

NLP refers to a whole series of 'perceptual positions' and these have been illustrated in Chapter 3. The point of considering these positions is to understand better how others view situations and react to them. You might like to have a go at using different perspectives in the following situations:

★ **Shopping:** If you have to stand in a queue, imagine that you are in the position of the shop assistant (ie take on what is called 'second position'). This will give you an idea of what is going on for that person. Then imagine what it is like for the person behind you in the queue (a further 'second-position' shift). Then imagine how the entire queue looks to other people wandering around the shop (taking on 'third, or meta, position'). Each time you shift perspective in this way it can give you an insight into other people's situations and responses.

★ **Family occasions:** If you bring a new visitor to meet members of your family, imagine taking on the perspectives of the individual members of your family ('second position') and think how your friend might appear to them, then consider how your family might come across to your friend (adopting 'second position' in relation to your friend). Then, finally, imagine how you, together with your family, come across to your friend (taking meta-position in relation to yourself and the family).

These differing perspectives can help you tune into other people's experience and help you see things in a new light. When you take on other people's perspectives, they are more likely to feel you understand them and be more responsive to your dealings with them.

Creating and Maintaining Rapport

You will probably be aware that there are some people with whom you feel really at ease and others to whom you find it harder to relate. Sometimes you can meet someone for the first time and immediately feel comfortable with them, as if you had known them for years. What is it that makes the difference?

When people are getting on well together, we say they are 'in rapport'. NLP offers a simple way of thinking about rapport. The principle is that people tend to get on well with others who are similar to them in some way, for example people who share similar interests, live in similar houses, like similar food or music, wear similar clothes or think in similar ways. The idea behind this is that if you look in a mirror you see something familiar, and if someone looks at you and sees something similar, it is familiar and not threatening, therefore making yourself similar in some ways tends to make you seem more acceptable.

A key NLP process is that of creating and maintaining rapport with others and there are some easy ways to help this along. The underlying principle is that if you do not have automatic rapport with someone, you can create it by making yourself like that person in some way or fitting in with what they do, for example by talking about an activity you know they like or by being quiet if they are trying to study.

There are different ways in which you can try to be like another person. One way is to mimic them. Mimicking is often very badly received, however, as it can result in the person feeling ridiculed or embarrassed. A second way in which you can make yourself like another person is to mirror them. This means doing exactly as they do. Mirroring can be very obvious and overdone, however. A better process is what NLP calls 'matching'. Matching means doing some things in a similar way to the other person, but doing the *minimum* necessary to make yourself like them, not the maximum.

Let's take an example of mimicking, mirroring and matching to see how they work out in practice. Suppose you are in a railway train, in a corner seat near a window, and sitting opposite you, also in a corner seat, is another person. The other person is leaning to one side, with legs crossed, tapping one toe up and down constantly, occasionally glancing out of the window.

If you were going to mimic the person, you might tap your foot up and down in the same way. This could result in the person getting irritated. If you mirrored them, you might sit in exactly the same position, leaning to the side, with your legs crossed. This would probably involve unnecessary complication. To match them, you might simply adopt a similarly relaxed posture, not necessarily identical, but relaxed rather than tense. Or, each time the other person looks out of the window, you might do so (a few seconds later in order to make it less obvious) or, instead of looking out of the window, you might glance along the carriage. These are ways of being similar without copying exactly. Have a go at this yourself the next time you are travelling.

Matching is a natural process; when people are getting on well together they naturally do things in a synchronized way. Just look at couples walking along the street together and notice that they are generally taking steps at the same time as each other. If you match other people, they are more likely to feel at ease with you.

I have talked about matching posture, movement and gestures, but there are many other things which can be matched, for example thought processes. If you are with someone who always thinks long term, you could talk to them about long-term issues, rather than short-term ones. If you are with someone who is making mental images of plants for their garden, you could talk in graphic terms about other plans so the person could see these too in their 'mind's eye'. What you are doing in these instances is considering how the other person is thinking, either in relation to the concepts they are using or to how their mind is creating their thoughts, and then matching their thought processes.

You can also match people's emotional state. If you are with someone who is upset, they will probably feel better if you talk quietly and don't overwhelm them with fast movements and gestures; if you are with someone who is excited, they will probably respond better if you also demonstrate excitement rather than detachment.

An important element of matching is to maintain what NLP refers to as 'congruence', ie consistency in what you do. If, for example, you were asked what you thought of an event and you said you thought it went well while at the same time shaking your head, the other person would receive a mixed message. Congruence is about selecting your actions or responses and then making sure they are consistent with each other.

Finally, there may be times when matching would not be helpful, for example if someone is taking up too much of your time and you want them to leave you in peace, when a discussion has reached a stalemate and there needs to be a change in energy, or where you are being harassed and wish to bring the interaction to a speedy end. In such cases, 'mis-matching', ie doing the opposite of what the other person is doing, is probably a better process to engage in.

Using Language Flexibly

A major feature of relating to others is the way in which language is used to communicate. Each language has its own unique characteristics and each individual person has their own unique way of using words. Because of this diversity in communication, it is essential to be able to exercise flexibility in how one uses words, so that communication can be geared very specifically to the person, or people, concerned.

NLP has much to offer the serious communicator. We have already discussed some of the non-verbal elements involved in relating to others; the next section will give you some ways of using words more effectively in your interactions with different people.

NLP has two basic language models, as mentioned in Chapter 2. The first model is called the Meta-Model and originated from the work of Richard Bandler and John Grinder. The second model is called the Milton Model and is based on the way in which Milton Erickson, a well-known psychiatrist and hypnotherapist, conducted his interactions with his clients. As with the Meta-Model, these patterns were described by Richard Bandler and John Grinder as they studied the way in which Dr Erickson worked.

The Meta-Model gives ways of being precise with language in order to achieve clarity of communication and understanding; the Milton Model relies heavily on suggestion, indirect language, metaphor and implied directions. These models are enormously useful in both day-to-day interactions and professional activities.

If you want to deal with others more effectively, it can help to use both the Meta-Model and the Milton Model appropriately. Let's take some day-to-day occurrences and see how the use of one or other model can help or hinder your communication.

Car Maintenance

Suppose your car has developed a fault and you wish to have it sorted out by your local garage. Here are two possible conversations you might have:

Car mechanic: *'What's the problem?'*
You: *'The car's making some kind of noise from time to time. It seems to be coming from the back.'*

Car mechanic: *'What's the problem?'*
You: *'There's a loud grating noise which seems to be coming from the near side, towards the back. I can hear it when I put the brakes on, but only when the car is very warm.'*

The first description is Milton Model language: non-specific. Listen to some of the words: 'some kind of noise', 'from time to time', 'from the back'.

The second description is Meta-Model language: much more precise. These words include 'loud', 'grating', 'near side, towards the back', 'when I put the brakes on', 'only when the car is very warm'.

In a situation where precise information is required, Meta-Model language is most useful, making things clearer for the other person.

Health

Take another situation, a visit to the doctor.

Doctor: *'What's the problem?'*
Patient: *'I feel a bit under the weather. I keep having aches and pains and I'm not my usual self.'*

Doctor: *'What's the problem?'*
Patient: *'I've had a stomach ache for the past two days. I've also had a headache since this morning and I felt very queasy when I woke this morning.'*

Again, the doctor is more likely to be able to help the patient if the information given is clear and concise.

Now contrast these two examples with a different situation.

Education

A teacher is giving a class some homework to do.

Teacher: *'I'd like you to write an essay about your last holiday. Say where you went, what you did, the things you enjoyed and the people you met.'*

Teacher: *'I'd like you to produce something on a recent holiday. There are lots of interesting things about holidays – places, people, activities and so on. You can think about what you would like to include, such as your feelings about the holiday, things you learned and so on.'*

In the first of these examples, the teacher made the task very prescriptive, saying things such as 'write' and 'say where you went' (using precise Meta-Model type language). In the second example, the teacher left a lot to the imagination of each individual pupil, saying things like 'produce something', 'interesting things', 'what you would like to include'. Using Milton Model language, it is possible to encourage people to think for themselves, be creative and innovative and consider their own personal approach to tasks. Using Meta-Model language is likely to limit such activity and may result in forcing a narrower response.

Being Persuasive and Influential

The final topic we will cover in this chapter is persuasion and influence. Long before NLP had a name, there were world-famous writers producing books on how to 'win friends and influence people'. Now self-help and influencing skills are extremely common topics in NLP books and many of the most notable current writers and speakers on NLP concentrate on helping people to promote themselves and their services or products through persuasion and influence.

It is worth adding here that when persuasion and influence are mentioned, people sometimes feel that what is really being discussed is manipulation. As already outlined in Chapter 1, NLP is neutral as a process. Of course, manipulation is possible in any situation but, if the approach of the person initiating the action is ethical, then this is unlikely to occur. And, as mentioned previously, NLP practitioners generally do have respect for those with whom they come into contact; this is instilled at an early stage in their training.

Many of the skills which underlie influencing people have already been covered in this chapter: using observation skills, shifting perspective, creating rapport and using language effectively. All these elements need to be in place before attempting to influence someone; if you do not observe the situation, consider the other person's position and create an effective relationship with them, it is unlikely that you will be able to influence them significantly. Once you have established these foundations, however, you can take things further.

So, what are the additional elements which are involved in influencing others? I will consider six points here:

★ using the other person's motivational patterns to establish credibility and stimulate enthusiasm
★ reinforcing verbal messages non-verbally

★ using metaphor to create understanding
★ moving conversations into the future
★ using the person's preferred ways of perceiving to enhance your message
★ providing evidence to meet the other person's requirements

Using Motivational Patterns

To hold someone's interest, it helps to know what motivates them. One way of finding this out is through their language patterns. Psychometric tests work on the principle that it is possible, through questioning, to elicit people's underlying personality and motivational traits, but it is also possible to get similar information just through normal conversation. In NLP, these traits are referred to as 'Meta-Programmes' and there are several common ones which can easily be elicited.

Let's take just one of the motivational patterns which can be evoked. This pattern is to do with a person's strength of belief in their own views, opinions and ways of doing things. A person who has strong views and defends them passionately can be termed 'internal'. The opposite is 'external', the term used to refer to a person who frequently needs feedback and endorsement.

You can find out whether a person is internal or external by asking some simple questions, but do remember that these traits are related to circumstances and can change over time, so that someone can be internal at work and external in relationships, or external when very young but more internal as time passes. To assess internal or external orientation, good questions to ask are: 'How do you know you have done a good job at work?' or 'How do you know you have decorated a room well?' An internal person will say something like 'I just know I've done a good job' or 'I can see the results I have achieved', whereas an external person may say 'My boss tells me' or 'People say how nice it looks.'

Once you know a person's motivational pattern you can match their pattern in order to influence them. So to influence an internal person you might say 'You will know how important it is to be on time' and to influence an external person you might say 'I would really like you to be there on time.'

For more information on this kind of influencing process, do read Shelle Rose Charvet's excellent book *Words that Change Minds*, also *People Pattern Power* by Marilyne and Wyatt Woodsmall *(see Bibliography)*, and look at the LAB (Language and Behaviour) Profile, a questionnaire designed by Rodger Bailey to elicit a number of Meta-Programmes which relate to people's motivational patterns.

Re-enforcing Verbal Messages Non-verbally

NLP has a term for non-verbal support to messages: 'analogue marking'. Analogue markings are usually gestures, although they could also be voice tonality and vocal emphasis. Reinforcing verbal messages can lend weight to your arguments. One way of doing this is by using hand gestures to demonstrate what you mean, for example moving your hands apart to show that something is a *big* issue. Another way is to emphasize part of a sentence by saying the words louder or emphasizing them in some other way to indicate its importance, for example 'Please *keep off* the grass.'

Using Metaphor to Enhance Understanding

Our unconscious minds frequently work with metaphor. This can be noted, for example, in dreams, where everyday and familiar people, places and events may take on distorted forms. The English language is incredibly full of metaphor – that phrase itself is a metaphor, of course, as language cannot actually *be full* of anything, as it is not a container! You might notice that organizations have their own corporate metaphors, such as sporting analogies, for example 'We should all *pull together*', or gardening analogies, for example 'Things are really *blossoming* at the moment.'

By using metaphor, you can influence people at many levels and it really helps to *match* their own metaphors where possible. So if someone says that looking after their disabled aunt is an *uphill struggle* you can respond: 'And when you are going uphill, it can be wonderful to find places to rest and enjoy the view before continuing.' You have taken their language and used it to reply. Your reply may then influence them to consider taking a rest.

Moving Conversations into the Future

This is an interesting concept. People often find it hard to make decisions or take action because they are stuck in the past or immersed in the present. Giving them a sense of the future can provide an incentive to move on. This can be done simply by using future tenses, an approach which comes from the NLP language models, in particular the Milton Model (*see Chapter 3*). So, for example, you can say things like '*When* you use this', '*Once* you have done that', and so on. Giving people an experience of the future can be powerfully influential.

Using Preferred Ways of Perceiving

I have already spoken about the different senses people use (sight, sound, touch, taste, smell). Many people use all their senses to a high degree, but some seem to favour one or more in particular. Some people are highly 'visual', such as designers, others are very 'kinaesthetic', for example dancers, and some are very 'auditory', for example musicians. If you wish to influence someone to move in a new direction, it may be that you need to help them develop the use of senses which have been somewhat dormant.

For example, if you want to help someone furnish a room comfortably, but they are very auditory and don't have a highly kinaesthetic sense, you could start by *matching* their auditory preference by discussing how the room would sound with different furniture and then *lead* them into a more tactile awareness. So you might say: 'Just imagine how it would sound with polished floorboards; your shoes would make a really loud noise as you walked [*auditory*]. With soft carpet, however, it would muffle the sound [*auditory*]. Just imagine how that soft carpet would feel [*kinaesthetic*] and how good it would feel [*kinaesthetic*] to just let your feet sink into that softness [*kinaesthetic*].'

What you have done is to move the person into feelings from sounds, influencing them to have a new kind of experience.

Providing Evidence to Meet their Requirements

Finally, if you wish to influence someone, it helps to show that it will be beneficial for them. One way of doing this is what NLP calls Evidence of Fulfilment (sometimes known as Complex Equivalence). What this is about is the fact that when people have a belief, they also have things which, for them, are evidence for that belief. For example, if someone's leg has been bitten by a mosquito and swollen up, the person might think that mosquitoes are dangerous to everyone. It could, however, be that the person is extremely allergic to mosquito bites and the reaction is more to do with them than the mosquito. Showing them that they are allergic, whereas other people are not, is the 'evidence' that could alter their perception of the situation.

So, if you can provide evidence that differs from what a person previously had in their mind, there is a good chance they will alter their opinions. But to do that, you have to know what their existing Evidence of Fulfilment is.

As an example of such evidence, suppose you would like to go out for a meal with a friend, but the response you get to an invitation is: 'It's too much effort just now.' To find out what this means to the person (their evidence), you could ask: 'How is it too much effort just now?'

The person might reply: 'It means changing clothes and driving the car.' You might then say: 'Well, we could go somewhere informal where you don't need to dress up, and I can drive the car.' This works with the person's own beliefs about the situation and shows that their needs can be met.

This section has given you some ideas about persuasion and influence. NLP has much to offer in this area, helping you relate well to friends, acquaintances, partners, service providers and others. And creating and maintaining good social relationships can have effects on other areas of your life. It may enable you to feel more confident and self-assured; it may alleviate stress caused by conflict and disagreement; it may bring you more opportunities through extending the circle of people with whom you build contacts and interact.

It is well worth exploring further, but do remember to take other people's wishes and needs into account as well as your own when you are using influencing skills. Achieving 'win-win' situations benefits both parties.

Chapter 6

Work and Business

The last two chapters have been about ways of enhancing personal performance; this chapter moves into the world of work and considers how NLP can enhance work performance and relationships. Although NLP began life through the study of therapists, it is now commonly used as a business development tool and can offer effective, rapid and stimulating ways of enhancing business skills and performance.

What are the common issues for many people at work? The following are ones which are probably familiar to you:

★ setting objectives
★ planning and organizing
★ solving problems and making decisions
★ managing time, finance and other resources
★ dealing with, and managing, others, including negotiating, interviewing, counselling, appraising, running meetings and teambuilding
★ training, facilitating, coaching and mentoring
★ writing letters, memos and reports
★ making presentations/public speaking
★ carrying out research and development

★ being innovative
★ selling and marketing
★ customer care
★ personal professional development

All these areas are ones which are required across a range of work and business situations and NLP can provide ways of making them all simpler and more enjoyable. There are many NLP books on specialist areas of business, particularly selling, negotiating, managing time, training, creativity and teambuilding and some of these are mentioned in the Bibliography.

This chapter will take a few work and business-related topics and show how the application of NLP can improve personal and group success. The topics we will be covering in some depth are:

★ objective setting
★ time management
★ planning and organizing
★ negotiating
★ Continuing Professional Development (CPD)

At the end of the chapter we will consider how NLP can be applied to the other business topics mentioned above.

Objective Setting

In your work, you will probably have found that it is easier to achieve results if you have a clear idea of what you are aiming for (and if you don't undertake paid work, you can still apply the following concepts to many other activities). There is a commonly used business acronym, SMART, which stands for five things which are useful in objective setting; the letters represent:

★ Specific
★ Measurable
★ Achievable
★ Realistic
★ Time based

All these things are important in objective setting and NLP has taken this process further with what is called 'Well Formedness'. In NLP, people are encouraged to strive for what are termed 'Well Formed Outcomes' or WFO for short *(see also Chapter 1)*.

There are several elements to the Well Formedness model and those most commonly described are:

Stating what you want in a positive manner

The principle behind this is that objectives should be stated positively rather than negatively. So, for example, when shopping, most people tend to make lists of the things they want to buy, rather than the things they wish to avoid. It is extremely hard to work towards a goal which is stated negatively, for example, 'I don't want to be anxious when making a presentation.' Once you know how you do want to be in presentations, for example confident and calm, you stand a better chance of working towards your goal and then achieving it.

Thinking about the context surrounding what you want to achieve

This means that it helps to define where and when and how you wish your objective to apply. For example, if you want to arrange a meeting, it helps to define which people need to be there, where it will be held, the duration of the event, who will lead and record it and the degree of formality that is required.

Striving to achieve the appropriate level of result

When an objective is set, it is important to know the target to be aimed for and to check that it is the 'real' target, rather than simply a step on the way. So, if you want to improve the productivity of a work unit, the level of result targeted might include the percentage increase required and the quality required. You will need to check that the level is not set too high, so you have too much of the product left over, and not too low, so that you have too little to distribute. Equally, it is important to check that the real objective is the productivity increase, rather than, for example, enhancing your image in the eyes of senior management. If the real objective is different, there may be better ways of achieving it.

Working out the advantages and disadvantages

This might seem self-explanatory, but the NLP approach here is to consider what are called 'secondary gains'. The idea of secondary gains is that people often gain hidden benefits from situations remaining unchanged. An objective could be to improve job clarity and make job descriptions more detailed and explicit. However, a hidden benefit in not doing this could be that people take on tasks which are not always defined and if job descriptions were tightened up, it could stifle flexibility and innovation. So, when considering your objective, do work out whether there are any negative consequences of making the change and any hidden benefits in staying as you are.

Considering the 'ecology', or the circumstances surrounding the goal

'Ecology' is a term commonly used in NLP; it concerns the need to check that decisions or changes are appropriate. To this end, it is important to consider the feasibility of the steps to be taken, whether the objective is actually achievable, whether what is planned is in accordance with other elements of the situation, such as cultural traditions/norms and the personal beliefs and attitudes of those involved.

Being able to measure results

This is another important element and relates to both measurement and standards. If you do not know how to assess the results of your effort, it becomes hard to set an effective objective. If you say, for example, that you wish to be better organized, this is a very vague objective. Once you begin to define it in terms of measures, or assessments, things improve. So two measures of 'being better organized' could be keeping your desktop clear (which you can assess by whether or not you can see any papers on it) and managing your time better (which you could measure by the amount of time you spend in unnecessary activities and also by the number of people who tell you your time is well spent). The rather different element which NLP brings to measurement is more personal measures, such as what you can see, hear and feel once you achieve results, as well as purely statistical measurements.

Assessing the degree of control you actually have

This is an interesting point, and one with which NLP is much concerned. People often aspire to things which are beyond their control, for example other people behaving in a particular way. It is possible, for example, to say you would like someone to stop being aggressive towards you, but this is unlikely to be within your control. Better to say you would like to be able to handle the person's aggression so you can respond to it in a positive manner; this is within your control and more likely, therefore, to be achieved. And, of course, by exercising control over your own responses, it is much more likely that the other person will be influenced to respond in a different way.

Gathering the resources required

It is difficult to achieve an objective without adequate resources and the most obvious resources at work include time, money, equipment and people. In NLP, however, there are other resources which need to be considered. These include personal skills and experience; they also include positive beliefs and attitudes, confidence, motivation and similar elements of thought and feeling.

Knowing yourself

Last on this list, but not least. The importance of an objective being in keeping with a person's self-concept and personal values is vital. If you try to achieve something because you are told you should, because others achieve that thing or because you feel it is what you ought to be doing, there is less chance of it being successful. So self-analysis and awareness are key to achieving results. *(See Chapter 4 for more on developing self-awareness.)*

Time Management

We all have the same amount of time each day – 24 hours – yet:

★ some people manage to achieve a good deal in that time and others achieve less

★ some people find the time passes rapidly and others find it passes slowly
★ some people feel overwhelmed by what they have to do in that time, while others feel they have all the time in the world for their tasks

What makes the difference?

This is where NLP offers more than conventional time-management training. Time-management skills are simple to learn and straight-forward to apply, yet many people do not apply them. This is probably because what counts is not just knowing the techniques to use, but having the motivation to use them. NLP can help you focus on your attitudes to time management and also your perception of time.

Attitudes towards Time

Try a small test. Look at your desk, if you have one. See if there are any items there which need dealing with, but which remain untouched. Now consider any messages these deferred tasks are sending you. For each postponed activity, there is probably an associated communica-tion. Do any of these sound familiar?

★ 'You don't like dealing with me.'
★ 'You find me boring.'
★ 'You don't know where or how to start with me.'
★ 'You don't think you can handle me.'
★ 'Last time you dealt with me you messed things up.'

Now it is possible that the only reason some of your tasks have not been completed is because you genuinely have not had time to do them. It is also likely that some of them will have been set aside for one of the reasons above, or something similar. In other words, it is your attitudes towards the tasks, your beliefs about them, or thoughts and feelings in connection with them which has prevented you from doing them.

With NLP you can analyse your attitudes, beliefs, thoughts and feelings in order to find out how they are affecting your behaviour and thereby your achievements. *(See the section on the Experiential Array in Chapter 1 for more on this.)* Unless you tackle some of these issues it is unlikely that you will have the motivation and perseverance to start and complete the necessary tasks.

So, find out what message each of the unfinished tasks is sending you and then ask yourself some questions about the task, such as: 'Do I want to do this?', 'Do I need to do this?' and 'Is this worth doing?'

Once you have your answers to the questions, you can decide whether to tackle the task and, if you do decide to go ahead with it, NLP can offer you ways of getting there.

Taking the five bullet points above, let us see how NLP can help.

Not liking a task

If you do not like *doing* a task, you could imagine *having done it*. This shifts your perspective into a future time, after it has been done, when you can picture it completed and imagine how good you will feel now it is finished. To do this, you can use visualization to picture the task successfully completed.

Finding it boring

With this one, you can search for a challenge in the task, such as seeing how quickly you could complete it. An alternative would be to give yourself a reward for working on the task for a specific length of time – you could then look forward to the reward instead of avoiding the task.

Not knowing where to start

Here, you can use the 'chunking' technique described below under 'Planning and Organizing' to sort the activity into its component elements and see it in context. Once you have read the following section you can return to this item, knowing more about the technique which can be applied.

Thinking you can't handle it

This may be to do with self-concept and the techniques I discussed in Chapter 4, on self-esteem, could help here. Using positive 'internal dialogue' can really help in boosting your confidence. Alternatively, you could think of situations in the past where you *have* handled equally challenging tasks successfully and use them to boost your belief in your capabilities.

Being concerned about doing it badly

By thinking in this way, you are focusing on what you do not want to happen, rather than on what you would like as a positive result. As we saw when considering objectives, the first important thing is to be able to specify your targets in a positive manner. So two things come in here: the first is the focus on avoidance and the second is how your mind recalls a previous experience of things not going well. To tackle the first, you can refocus yourself on the positive things you could do to ensure success. To tackle the second, you can work on changing your mental images, sounds or feelings to positive ones instead of negative, as I have illustrated previously.

Perception of Time

NLP can help give you the sense of having more time available to complete what you have to do. Think about being stuck in a traffic jam, being in the dentist's chair or having to wait for a much-anticipated letter. How quickly does time pass for you in these situations? Now think about how time passes at weekends, at times when you are reading a good book or when you are taking part in an exciting activity. How fast does time go now? Probably your perception of the passage of time differs between the first kind of activity and the second time. Everyone has their own situations where time seems to drag on interminably and situations where things seem to be over in a flash. Being able to change your perception of time so that it apparently slows down can reduce any sense of pressure and make you feel more relaxed about what you have to do.

So what makes the difference between time passing quickly or slowly?

The only thing that changes is your own perception of the time as it passes (or, in many cases, your lack of perception of the time as it passes). As the time passes, your mind is doing things such as showing you pictures, producing sounds and giving you feelings, and these will be different for situations which you regard as 'interesting' or 'exciting' and those which you regard as 'dull and tedious'.

In *The Dance of Life* (Anchor Books, New York, 1983), a fascinating book about the nature of time, E. T. Hall describes an experiment by Alton de Long into the perception of time. In the experiment, people were asked to sit in front of miniaturized environments (like a doll's house room), imagine they were a figure in that environment carrying out some activity and then tell the experimenters when half an hour had passed. The curious thing is that their perception of time related directly to the reduction in size of their environment, so that in a twelfth size environment they perceived that half an hour had passed in 2.44 minutes and in a twenty-fourth size environment they perceived half an hour to have passed in 1.36 minutes. Hall deduced:

Time and space are functionally interrelated ... the perception of time is ... also influenced by the scale of the environment ... under proper conditions, subjects will increase interaction rates in an environment to stay in agreement with the scale of that environment ... the brain speeds up in direct proportion to environmental scale.

It would appear, according to Hall, that it should be possible to accomplish certain kinds of decision-making tasks in an enormously reduced time, as well as giving an individual up to 12 hours' experience in the course of an hour!

So perception of time is not a fixed element, but can vary according to both the attitudes of the person and the environment in which the person is functioning.

NLP has many ways of working with perception of time and two of the best known are:

★ time lines
★ time distortion

Time Lines

The idea of 'time lines' (a very old concept, as mentioned in Chapter 3) is that people are able to distinguish between events happening in the past, present and future not only cognitively, but also representationally. In Chapter 3 we considered the possibility of being able to review situations from different points in time; in this chapter we will extend this approach into how you, as an individual, represent time to yourself. Have a go at the following exercise to demonstrate how this can come about.

Think about a particular event which occurred some time ago, say five or ten years. Choose an event which left a lasting memory (choose a pleasant event rather than unpleasant one for the purposes of this exercise). As you think of the event, notice whether your attention is drawn in any particular direction (to one side of yourself, in front or behind you, high up or low down and so forth) or whether your focus of attention is internal (inside your head). Repeat this process, thinking first of another memorable event in the more recent past (say a few days ago), then an event which is likely to occur in the next few days and finally an event which is likely to take place some years hence. In each case, notice where your attention is drawn.

Once you have a location for each event, draw an imaginary line joining them all up. Each person will have a unique way of representing these connections and it has been noticed that there are some common ways. The most common are lines which are out in front of a person (say from left to right) and lines which run 'through' a person (generally from front to back). NLP calls the first pattern 'through time' and the second pattern 'in time'.

As far as time management goes, it seems that 'through time' people, ie those who 'perceive' time as if it is visible in front of them, tend to be well organized, aware of time as it passes, punctual and reliable. 'In time' people are immersed in time; for them, past, present and future are all interconnected and they tend to be less aware of the passage of time and less concerned with its significance; they may be late for appointments and find it hard to complete tasks to schedule.

So, if you wish to improve your time management, it helps to become more aware of the tasks and activities you have to do as external to yourself and, where possible, to 'see' them in front of you, noticing their component parts, how they relate to other tasks you have to undertake and so forth. By giving projects a kind of embodiment, making them tangible, it is easier to get a sense of how long they will take to do and how to approach them.

Time Distortion

This is a technique which is much used in hypnotherapy and NLP therapists find it a useful way of assisting people to feel as though they have more time when under pressure and, conversely, have time speeded up on occasions when it could potentially drag, such as going to the dentist or waiting in a traffic jam. This is not an appropriate technique to cover in depth in an introductory book, but the process consists of getting into a highly relaxed state and then giving yourself suggestions (or, more usually, being given them by a therapist) that time is passing either faster or slower. The suggestions are usually given in the context of a particular scenario – for example you might be asked to imagine how slowly time seems to pass when you are waiting in a supermarket queue and then be helped to transfer that feeling of time slowing down into a work situation when you need more time to complete a task. These techniques are extremely effective (and similar to ones that are used for the control of perception of pain). If you wish to know more, NLP psychotherapists are the people to contact *(see Useful Addresses)*.

Planning and Organizing

All of us need to plan at some time in our lives. Having techniques to help with this process is a great aid to effectiveness.

An NLP technique which is very helpful in planning and organizing is called 'chunking' *(this was covered briefly in Chapter 3)*. Chunking is a process whereby activities may be analysed and tackled in a systematic way. Using chunking, it is possible to see any activity in its full context. Let's take an example of a work issue and see how chunking could be applied to it.

Suppose you have to plan and organize a meeting concerned with an office relocation. Let us represent the meeting as a box, shown below:

```
┌─────────────────────────┐
│      Meeting on         │
│  office re-location     │
└─────────────────────────┘
```

It could be easy to see the meeting out of context, ie as a self-contained event. However, the meeting is only one event in the relocation process. Because the overall process is bigger than the meeting, we can add it, above the original box, to our diagram as follows:

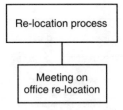

Now let us consider the meeting in a broader context. This meeting is on relocation, but other meetings may need to take place on general business finance and on competition from other businesses. These meetings are equivalent in significance to the relocation meeting and can, therefore be added to the diagram at the same level, as follows:

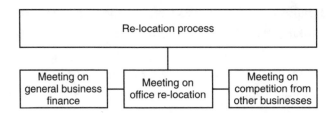

Finally, let us take the meeting itself and consider what elements it comprises. Some components of the meeting could be as follows:

★ the people to be invited
★ the time the meeting is to be held
★ the venue for the meeting
★ the documentation required
★ the refreshments to be provided
★ how minutes will be taken

All these are sub-elements of the meeting and can also be added to the diagram as sub-parts as follows:

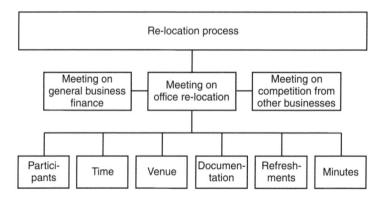

So the diagram we now have puts the meeting in its total context.

The chunking process allows you to think about the component elements of any situation and to represent them in diagrammatic form. Once you have analysed them in this way, it becomes easier to see interrelationships and to break down the activities you need to complete.

Negotiating

There are many work situations where negotiation is necessary. Some people are professional negotiators, for example involved in industrial relations, estate agency or car sales. Others simply negotiate as part of their everyday work activities – negotiating lunchtime cover for themselves, negotiating more time to prepare a report, negotiating their salary level and so forth. For all these situations, there are NLP techniques which can facilitate acceptable outcomes.

Rackham and Carlisle (*Journal of European Industrial Training*, 1978) described the characteristics of effective negotiators. One of the characteristics was the ability to predict objections, changes of mind or other obstacles to successful implementation and to take action early on to forestall them. NLP has a term for dealing with such events: 'future pacing'. Future pacing involves considering future scenarios in an effort to both predict and successfully handle them. Let us take a negotiating situation and see how future pacing might help it.

Suppose you are responsible for getting together a working party to see through a project. You know what has to be done and simply have to make sure you have the right people for the task. You need five people and can select from ten available. The ten are as follows (some of the descriptions below are loosely based on Meredith Belbin's team roles work and some take into account the NLP Meta-Programme categories):

1. Very bright, fast, energetic; tends to dominate meetings and bulldoze people who do not work at the same speed
2. Very good at detail, reliable and good at spotting mistakes; tends to hold things up while checking minor points
3. Good at seeing the 'big picture'; does not like having to work on fine detail

4. Excellent at dealing with others, networking and getting information; tends to spend a lot of time chatting and exploring options
5. Always comes up with good ideas; sometimes a bit too off the wall
6. Good at keeping everyone focused on the job in hand; sometimes ignores other options which could be even more helpful
7. A good technical person who knows about the subject area in question; not so good at understanding others' interests and involvement
8. Very positive and goal-focused; sometimes does not see obstacles in the way
9. A good time manager; sometimes takes short cuts in order to keep to schedule
10. Good at finding resources, sources of information and supplies; sometimes keener on the hunt for material than on the job in hand

Now, using future pacing, you could predict outcomes for different combinations of people on your project and think through what would happen with different groupings. For example:

★ What if I had the quick thinker, the person taking an overview and the contact person, together with the detail person and the technical expert? How would they get on and what would I have to do to keep them all together? How would it feel to be part of that group? Would we meet our timescales or would we be held up by internal conflict?
★ If I have the ideas person in the group, will it help or hinder? How would the others handle the more outrageous suggestions produced by that person?
★ Would the addition of a networking person be an asset? Would that person spend too much time on creating relationships inside and outside the group rather than getting on with the job?

What future pacing adds to this kind of assessment is the ability to imagine the future 'as if you are in it right now'. So, you can imagine how it would feel to be in meetings with the particular grouping of people you have in mind, you can imagine hearing the kind of conversations that would go on and you can imagine what will or will not get done as a result.

So, future pacing can help you answer questions such as: 'Is it appropriate to take this course of action?', 'What would it actually be like in that situation?', 'How will people respond?' and so forth. An NLP question to remember when considering the future is: 'Is it ecological?' – in other words, do all the elements involved work harmoniously, are they ethical and are all the components congruent (or consistent) with each other?

Personal Professional Development

Finally let us consider how you can extend your own personal development within a work context. Continuing Professional Development (CPD) is a term much in use at present. CPD is now a requirement which most professional bodies make of their members as they recognize the importance of keeping up with a rapidly changing business world. If you are keen to enhance your own professional knowledge and skills on a continuing basis, you may well be helped by NLP's emphasis on modelling, as mentioned in earlier chapters.

In a business context, modelling is about noticing which people are achieving excellent results and then adopting – in a modified form if necessary – some elements of what they do (specifically the elements which produce the difference between competence and *excellence* in performance).

As we saw in Chapter 1, NLP is concerned with the following elements of performance:

★ objectives
★ behaviour
★ mental strategy
★ emotional state
★ beliefs, values and assumptions

all operating within a specific context. If you wish to develop your own abilities, you can find out how high performers in your own field achieve their results by exploring their ways of dealing with each of these elements.

Let's take an example to illustrate how you might go about this. Suppose you want to promote an idea or product of yours. Now promotion is a process which has been going on for probably as long as human memory. Some things which have been promoted include religion, politics, travel, fitness, shampoo, evening papers, birdseed – you name it, someone has promoted it. This means there is a lot of expertise around concerning promotion, and it would be wasteful of time and energy to re-invent all the ideas and processes which have been generated.

This is where NLP's modelling techniques come in, helping you find out how people have done things before. So, to promote your own idea or product, find one or more people who you know are successful at promotional activities and begin to work out how they get their results. This is the process which Bandler and Grinder embarked upon in the early days of NLP.

To find out how these people act in such a successful way, you will need to ask them questions and/or observe them in operation. Here are some of the possible questions you might ask concerning the performance elements considered above:

Objectives

★ 'What do you want to *achieve* when you promote an idea/product?'

Behaviour

★ 'What do you *do* first when promoting something new?'
★ *'How* do you contact potential consumers?'
★ *'When* do you contact people? What time of day? What day of the week?'
★ *'What* do you *say* to them?'
★ 'Do you *telephone* them first?'
★ 'Do you *write to them*? If so, at what stage?'
★ 'When meeting potential consumers, how do you *behave*? What do you *wear*? How do you *speak*?'
★ 'What *posture* do you adopt? How do you *shake hands*?'
★ 'What kind of *promotional material* do you use? How does it *look*? What does it *say*?'

Mental strategy

★ 'What goes on *in your mind* as you consider promotional activities?'
★ 'Do you *visualize the outcome* you want?'
★ 'Do you *imagine* meetings with consumers going well?'
★ 'Do you *tell yourself* they will be interested?'
★ 'Do you *imagine hearing them* sounding interested?'

Emotional state

★ 'How do you *feel* when you consider promoting something?'
★ 'What *state* are you in just before meeting a potential consumer?'
★ 'What *state* are you in during the meeting/s?'
★ 'Do you *deliberately create a particular emotion* in yourself at any stage in the process? If so, *what is it*?'

★ 'How do you *feel* when you have been successful in a promotional activity?'

Beliefs, values and attitudes

★ 'What do you *believe* about the idea/product you are promoting?'
★ 'How *valuable* do you think the idea/product is?'
★ 'How *interested* do you think the consumer/s will be?'
★ 'What do you *believe* about your own ability to promote the idea/product?'
★ 'What is your *attitude* towards the consumer/s?'

Anything else?

★ 'Is there *anything else* you would like to tell me which is important to you about this process?'

This list of questions should give you an idea of how to approach the process of modelling. What you are aiming for is as complete a picture as you can get of how the person functions in this particular context and especially the elements that distinguish excellence from competence. If you can also observe the person in action, it is likely to be helpful. If you can question and observe several people in the same kind of situation, it should also give you an idea as to how approaches can vary and, importantly, what they have in common.

As an example, in a modelling project I carried out on management consultants in 1993, to find out about those who were good at converting business prospects into actual assignments, some *common features* of the most successful were:

★ They were much more proactive.
★ They were more client-centred than self-centred.

★ Their objectives were more to do with resolving problems and educating their clients, whereas the less effective ones' objectives were more to do with getting business and not wasting time.
★ They treated client interactions as partnerships, shared ventures and learning experiences.
★ They were more persistent and found the experience a personal challenge.
★ They had much more positive feelings, stressed the need to generate energy, to think positively and to respond to challenges.
★ They enjoyed dealing with their clients and said it was important to counter negative feelings and create 'the right frame of mind'. (In contrast, those who did not do so well felt exasperated by non-responding clients, felt the clients were 'useless and incompetent', felt negative and angry about them and said it wasn't worth the 'hassle' to deal with them.)
★ They were much more concerned with the big picture than with detail.
★ They kept better records of client contact.

So it is possible to build up a good picture of what makes for success and then, if appropriate, train yourself or others to achieve similar results.

NLP does not have the monopoly on role modelling, but because of its attention to the small 'chunks' of experience and perception, it has ways of defining excellence that are not often found elsewhere.

At the start of this chapter, we discussed various business-related topics and selected a small number to which NLP techniques could be applied. We have not explored all the topics mentioned, although some of them have been referred to briefly in other chapters of the book. There are many NLP techniques that can be used in all these business-related areas, and to remind you of some that can be useful, the following list is of other topics, together with some suggestions for NLP techniques you might use in each area:

★ **Problem solving and decision making:** These topics can be approached using chunking, TOTE diagrams, the Disney Strategy and future pacing.

★ **Dealing with and managing other people:** Useful techniques in this area include observation skills, rapport creation and maintenance, language skills, shifts of perspective and recognition of/respect for others' beliefs and values.

★ **Training, presenting, facilitating, coaching and mentoring:** Techniques you could consider include accelerated learning (identification of and responding to variation in learning styles), anchoring of positive states, use of indirect language and role modelling.

★ **Business writing:** This can be helped by matching readers' sensory preferences (using appropriate sensory-specific language, paper texture, graphics, etc.), matching their motivational patterns by using appropriate Meta-Programmes and influencing through the use of indirect language and embedded instructions.

★ **Research, development and innovation:** Helpful techniques could include the use of the Disney Strategy and time lines to generate ideas and evaluate options.

★ **Sales and marketing:** Results could be improved by considering customers' values and criteria in relation to products and services being promoted. Sales performance could be enhanced by generating positive thoughts and feelings before embarking on a sales activity.

★ **Customer care:** Here it is important to understand the customer's perspective, use language which makes the customer feel valued and listened to and maintain positive states in order to remain resourceful when dealing with criticism, hostility or disappointment.

Although there are many techniques you can use, if you are flexible you will be able to select approaches which work well for you whatever your own area of activity, and should improve your results as a consequence.

So, this final chapter has covered some techniques which can improve work performance. All the techniques are cross-contextual and likely to produce effects in more than one area of your life. So increasing your confidence can enhance your relationships, improving your relationships can make your working life easier and improving your business skills can give you more of a sense of achievement and self-worth. By using the techniques illustrated in these three applications chapters, you will be able to create a positive approach and achieve results in all areas of your life. As I said at the start, you have probably been 'doing NLP' already; the ideas in this book can help you continue to do it successfully and with enthusiasm.

Appendices

This section of the book is about practical ways in which you can pursue your interest in NLP if you choose to do so. You will find the following topics covered:

★ how to find out about training in NLP
★ how to contact others interested in, or involved with, NLP
★ a glossary of commonly used NLP terms
★ a bibliography
★ other useful resources, including magazines, videos and audiotapes
★ useful contact details to help you locate NLP organizations, find out about NLP training or find an NLP practitioner or therapist who can help with your personal needs

If you are new to NLP, you may find it easiest to have someone else help you learn and develop. Although many of the NLP processes are easy to explain in a book, others are more complex and it is helpful to have some guidance or support when working with them. It is also useful to have another person who can bring a different perspective to things; for example letting you know what they observe about you as you practise the various activities. If you do not have a friend or colleague who can help you, there are various established groups where you can find people with a similar interest in the topic.

Further Information

Training in NLP

There are various levels of training in NLP and these can seem a little puzzling to the beginner. Although most courses are not accredited by external agencies, there have recently been moves towards the availability of NVQ and MSc programmes in NLP. The types of training programme you are most likely to come across are as follows:

★ **Introductory Courses** These can take anything from a half day to a week. Sometimes a certificate is given which may count towards the next level of training

★ **Practitioner Training** A course providing training in the basic skills, knowledge and attitudes of NLP. Such courses may be anything from 7 to 20 days' duration, usually in a modular format and sometimes including distance learning elements. The Association for Neuro-Linguistic Programming used to recognize certain courses, but recognition is now not offered. Although short courses can be very effective, NLP requires substantial periods of practice and skills development which can really only be achieved either by longer courses or by courses with sufficient periods of time between study to enable integration and assimilation of what has been learned.

★ **Master Practitioner Training** An advanced course, building on the skills learned at Practitioner level. Also normally modular in format and of varying lengths and formats.

★ **Trainer Training** A more advanced level, aimed at those needing skills in training others.

If you are interested in undertaking training in NLP, an introductory course is recommended first, to see how you get on with the subject. You can then proceed to Practitioner training if you find it to your liking.

It is helpful to contact a range of organizations before deciding where to train and, where possible, to attend introductory evenings or workshops to get a feel for how different organizations work. Often introductory evenings are offered free of charge, or at very low cost, to give potential participants an understanding of how they function. The Association for Neuro-Linguistic Programming can provide a set of questions you can ask of organizations with which you are thinking of training; these will indicate how they work and what they offer.

Contact with Others Involved in NLP

If you are interested in NLP, but are not yet certain whether you would like to undertake formal training, there are a range of networking and practice groups around the UK which you can visit either free of charge or at very low cost. At these groups you can meet others with similar interests, hear speakers on different aspects of NLP and experience some of the NLP processes for yourself.

Information on UK and some overseas practice groups is given in ANLP's quarterly magazine *Rapport (see Bibliography)*.

Glossary of NLP Terms

This is a straightforward explanation of some commonly used NLP terms. Some of these words may be familiar to you from everyday usage, but NLP has occasionally given them different meanings, so please take this into account in reading the glossary.

Accessing cues

Movements or gestures that give an indication of the mental processes a person is using. Observation of external behaviour can help assess whether a person is using a particular sense (sight, hearing, touch, taste or smell) and the indicators for this include eye movements (or 'eye accessing cues') such as looking up when visualizing an image or looking down when experiencing a strong emotion, facial expression, hand gestures and bodily posture. The eyes have conventionally been the indicators most used to assess what is going on in a person's mind, however research (notably by Eric Robbie), has shown that other kinds of bodily activity can be used in a similar way to understand the fine detail (sub-modalities, *see page 165*) of how a person is thinking, such as whether they are making large or small pictures in their mind, or are seeing images in colour or black and white. Examples: If a person is making a large picture in their mind, they may lean back slightly as they try to encompass the size of the picture; if a person is visualizing how a word is spelled they may look up as they imagine how the word looks.

Acuity

Good observation skills. Examples: Noticing that someone's breathing has become faster; becoming aware of changes in voice tone as a person is speaking.

Analogue marking

Using a movement, gesture or vocal change to reinforce something that is said. Examples: Pointing to an object while mentioning it; saying: 'I would like you to go to the shops *now'* and making the word 'now' stand out by emphasizing it through a different voice tone.

Anchor

The association of a signal with a response. Examples: Hearing a tune and recalling a memory; wearing a business suit and feeling confident.

Association/dissociation

Being immersed in your feelings (association); being detached from yourself, as if you were an observer (dissociation). Examples: Listening to music and becoming absorbed in the experience (association); becoming aware of your tone of voice as you are speaking to someone (dissociation).

Auditory

Real or imagined use of the sense of hearing. Examples: Speaking on the telephone; imagining your own voice in your head.

Calibration

Observing the detail of a person's behaviour, including how they look and how they sound. These observations are then used as a reference base for further observations. Examples: If you have observed that a particular person's voice speeds up when they wish to end a phone conversation, on hearing the faster speed you may sense that they wish to draw the discussion to an end; if you have noticed that a person wrinkles their forehead when a discussion moves to a topic that does not interest them, you can make judgements about their interest in other subjects depending on whether or not they repeat this facial expression.

Chunking (up or down)

Taking either a broad view or a more detailed perspective in order to achieve a result. Examples: If two colleagues are in dispute about where to site a piece of office equipment, you can *chunk up* (or broaden the discussion) by asking them to consider how other people might also be affected by the decision; if a friend has become tired of how a room is decorated and wants to make a change, but doesn't know where to start, you could *chunk down* (get the person to focus on the detail, rather than the room as a whole) by asking what colour is preferred, how much money there is to spend and whether paper or paint is desired.

Congruence/incongruence

The presence of consistency (congruence) or absence of consistency (incongruence) in what a person says and/or does. Examples: Someone saying they dislike a particular food and, at the same time screwing up their face (congruence); someone telling you they have enjoyed a particular film at the same time as shaking their head (incongruence).

Criteria

Things which are important to people; what they value. Examples: 'When I choose a television I want it to have a *good design* [one criterion] and *be affordable* [another criterion]'; 'What is important to me in a job is *the responsibility I have* [one criterion] and *its distance from my home* [another criterion].'

Dissociation

See Association.

Ecology

Taking into account the circumstances, or context, surrounding an action, so that its appropriateness and impact may be assessed. Examples:

Taking into account the possible impact on a child's learning and circle of friends before deciding whether a house move should take place; considering whether the higher salary produced by a job change justifies the additional stress the job might generate.

Future pacing

Imagining how something will be in the future; trying it out in your mind. Examples: Visualizing a room painted yellow and thinking how your existing furniture will look in it; rehearsing a speech at a business event, as if the audience were already there and imagining how it will feel at the time.

Gustatory

The real or imagined use of the sense of taste. Examples: Tasting a biscuit as you eat it; imagining the taste of a biscuit.

Incongruence

See Congruence.

Kinaesthetic

The real or imagined use of the sense of touch and the real or imagined experience of emotion. Examples: Stroking a piece of velvet and feeling the softness of the fabric; remembering the feeling of excitement of winning a race.

Lead systems

The sense (sight, hearing, taste, touch or smell) which a person is most likely to utilize as an initial response to situations. The sense a person uses in this way can often be observed through their unconscious eye movements; it can also be assessed through their language (*see 'Predicates' below*). Examples: Considering making a speech and immediately picturing the audience that will be there (visual); wanting to go on holiday and having an instant sense of warm sunshine and sandy beaches (kinaesthetic). *See also 'Primary systems' below.*

Matching

Copying a small part of a person's behaviour. Matching helps develop rapport, as people tend to feel comfortable with someone who seems similar to themselves. Examples: Wearing formal clothes for an occasion when other people will be dressed similarly; smiling when a person smiles at you. Matching is sometimes referred to as 'mirroring', although this literally means copying exactly; this is unnecessary and can aggravate people, as can mimicking, where people may feel they are being ridiculed.

Meta

Denoting something which is beyond or above other things. In NLP the main uses of this term is in personal interactions and use of language. Examples: Meta-position, a perspective which is beyond an interaction, for example talking to someone while imagining being 'a fly on the wall'; Meta-state, a state beyond another state, for example feeling *angry* about being *afraid* of heights, or feeling *guilty* about being *lethargic*. (An NLP trainer/writer who expounds the practical use of meta-states is Michael Hall.)

Meta-Model/Milton Model

Two prominent NLP language models. The Meta-Model is about using language in a precise and explicit manner and the Milton Model is about using language in an indirect manner. Examples: 'It's easy to boil an egg; just cook it until it's the way you like it' (Milton Model language); 'To boil an egg you need to put the egg in a saucepan, completely cover the egg with cold water, bring it to the boil, turn the heat down until it simmers and wait three minutes until the egg is cooked through but still soft with a runny yolk' (Meta-Model language).

Meta-Programmes

Patterns of acting or reacting, which an individual tends to favour in given situations. Examples: Relying on your own opinions ('internal' Meta-Programme) rather than wanting feedback from others ('external' Meta-Programme); aiming for a goal ('towards' Meta-Programme) rather than avoiding an obstacle ('away from' Meta-Programme). Meta-Programmes may change across time and context, for any particular person.

Meta-States

A state above and beyond another state.

Milton Model

See Meta-Model

Mirroring

See Matching.

Modelling

Analysing and, if appropriate, copying – or helping someone else copy – another person's behaviour or way of being. Very useful in business performance, where top performers can be analysed and their skills taught to others. Examples: Observing someone chair a meeting effectively, working out what precisely they do to make it go well and then chairing a meeting in a similar way yourself; finding out how a person develops a feeling of confidence and using their approach to help others become confident also. Modelling can be carried out as 'deep-trance identification' or 'strategy modelling' *(see Chapter 3)*.

Olfactory

The real or imagined use of the sense of smell. Examples: Smelling a rose; remembering the smell of a rose.

Outcome

An objective you wish to attain or the actual results you are achieving. Examples: *Wanting* to ride a bicycle; missing a train and, as a result, *having more time* to sit on the platform and read a book.

Pacing

Continuing to match (*see 'Matching' above*) another person or people as they change their behaviour. Examples: Smiling when a friend tells you of a happy event and then having a more serious face as they tell you about a problem they are having; speeding up your voice when you talk to an angry customer who is speaking quickly on the telephone and then slowing your voice as the person calms down a little and begins to speak more slowly.

Perceptual positions

The different perspectives we can adopt when considering a situation. An infinite number of perceptual positions could exist, but three are generally described. Examples: Being so engrossed in an activity that you do not hear someone calling to you (being in *'first position'*, or totally 'in your own experience'); feeling a friend's anxiety on going to a job interview (being in *'second position'* or imagining what the other person's experience is like); thinking how you and the other members of your family seem as a group to visitors arriving for a meal (being in *'third position'*, sometimes called 'meta-position' as it is beyond the interaction itself, or imagining how you and the others seem to outside observers).

Predicates

Words that relate to the use of the different senses (sight, hearing, touch, taste, smell). Examples: Clear, bright (predicates of *sight*); loud, squeaky (predicates of hearing); heavy; smooth (predicates of *touch*); sweet, bitter (predicates of *taste*); acrid, musty (predicates of *smell*). *See also 'Representational systems' page 165.*

Presuppositions

Assumptions which may or may not be valid, but are used to inform behaviour. Examples: Asking: 'When are you going to see the film?' presupposes the person will see it at some stage; cooking a meal for visitors presupposes they will be prepared to eat it.

Primary systems

The sense (sight, hearing, touch, taste, smell) that a person tends to favour. Examples: needing to see the dessert trolley in a restaurant in order to decide what to choose could indicate that a person's lead system is visual; wanting to 'have a go', when assembling a new piece of equipment, rather than reading the instruction manual first, could indicate that a person's lead system is kinaesthetic/touch-related. *See also 'Lead systems' above.*

Rapport

A state which exists when people are getting on well with each other, often observable by the fact that some aspects of the people's behaviour are similar *(see 'Matching' page 161).* Examples: Two people walking down the street side by side and chatting in a friendly way are likely to be taking steps at the same pace as each other; it is often easier to share silence with someone when you are in rapport with them than when you are not.

Reframing

Taking a different perspective on a situation. Examples: Seeing a delay on your train as an opportunity to catch up on reading, rather than become annoyed; interpreting a critical comment as a helpful aid to improvement rather than as a negative action.

Representational systems

The five senses (sight, hearing, touch, taste, smell). NLP gives these senses particular names: *visual* (sight); *auditory* (hearing) (*auditory digital* is sometimes used as a term for the process of having imaginary conversations in one's head); *kinaesthetic* (touch and also emotional feeling); *gustatory* (taste); *olfactory* (smell). In NLP, the term 'representational systems' is often used to denote the *imagined* use of the senses, such as visualization or 'self-talk'. Examples: Visualizing yourself driving a new car; imagining the sound of a dog barking.

State

Usually regarded as the experiencing of a particular emotion. Examples: Being confident (a resourceful state); feeling depressed (generally a less resourceful state).

Sub-modalities

The elements of each sense. Examples: When visualizing something, we can make a mental picture which is large or small, colourful or dull, clear or hazy, still or moving (sense of sight); when imagining a sound we can imagine it as loud or quiet, sharp or muffled, intermittent or constant (sense of hearing).

Synaesthesia

The simultaneous experience of more than one sensory process ('synthesizing of the senses'). This may involve the representation of one sensory experience through a different channel or a representation in one sensory system eliciting an associated response in another system. Examples: 'Seeing' different colours when you hear different musical notes; having particular tastes in your mouth as you feel the shape of different objects.

Visual

The real or imagined use of the sense of sight. Examples: Looking at pictures in an exhibition; picturing, in your mind, what a tree will look like once its leaves have fallen off.

Bibliography and Other Resources

If you are interested in private study of NLP, or would just like to follow up this book with further exploration, the following should be of help. The items with an asterisk are probably the most approachable for the absolute beginner:

Books
Introductory

Introducing Neuro-Linguistic Programming – A good basic text, systematic and comprehensive (British). O'Connor and Seymour. Crucible. 1990.*

NLP: The New Technology of Achievement – Practical, serious, exploration of aspects of NLP. Andreas and Faulkner. Nicholas Brealey. 1996.

The Magic of NLP Demystified – An easy-to-read introduction to the subject. Lewis and Pucelik. Metamorphous Press. 1990.*

Unlimited Power – A popular exposition of many NLP concepts and techniques. Robbins. Simon and Schuster. 1988.*

Neuro-Linguistic Programming Volume 1: The Study of the Structure of Subjective Experience – An early text on NLP concepts. Dilts, Grinder, DeLozier. Meta Publications. 1978.

Frogs into Princes – The book that started it all; early NLP workshop transcripts. Bandler and Grinder. Real People Press. 1979.

Using your Brain for a Change – An introduction to sub-modalities. Entertaining introduction to the topic. Bandler. Real People Press. 1985.*

NLP: The Wild Days – A short personal account of NLP's origins. McClendon. Meta Publications. 1989.

An ABC of NLP – An easy-to-read guide to NLP terms and their applications. (British). Sinclair. Aspen. 1992.*

Meta-states: Managing the Higher Levels of Your Mind's Reflexivity –
 A presentation of an NLP model dealing with reflexivity and levels
 of mind. Hall. Neuro-Semantic Publications. 1995.

General

Leaves Before the Wind – Collected writings on NLP applications and
 developments. Bretto et al. Grinder, DeLozier and Associates. 1991.
Thinking Styles: Relationship Strategies That Work! – Identifying your
 own personal patterns. (British). Beddoes-Jones. BJA Associates Ltd.
 1999.*
In and Out the Garbage Pail – Fritz Perls' autobiography; lively, amusing
 and anecdotal. Perls. The Gestalt Journal Press. 1992 (1969 original
 publication).

New Code NLP

Turtles All the Way Down – Workshop transcripts introducing New
 Code approaches. DeLozier and Grinder. Grinder, DeLozier and
 Associates. 1987.

Training

Training with NLP – A practical guide for those in training and
 development (British). O'Connor and Seymour. Thorsons. 1994.
The Excellent Trainer – Information and activities for using NLP in
 training (British). Kamp. Gower. 1996.
40 Activities for Training with NLP – Looseleaf activities for trainers
 (British). Johnson. Gower. 1996.
The Creative Trainer – Accelerated learning techniques in training
 (British). Lawlor and Handley. McGraw Hill. 1996.

Language

Words that Change Minds: Influencing through the Use of Metaprogrammes
– Excellent guidance for those with or without experience in NLP.
Charvet. Kendall Hunt Publishing Co. Undated.*

People Pattern Power – Meta-Programmes via scenarios and dialogue.
Woodsmall and Woodsmall. International Research Unit for Human
Typological Studies. 1998.

The Structure of Magic (Volume 1): The Meta Model Explained – In-depth
exploration of linguistic processes. Bandler and Grinder. Science
and Behaviour Books. 1975. Also Volume 2.

Therapeutic Metaphors – An introduction to constructing and using
metaphors. Gordon. Meta Publications. 1978.

Metaphors in Mind: Transformation through Symbolic Modelling – 'Clean
Language' in practice (British). Lawley and Tompkins. The
Developing Company Press. 2000.

Business

NLP at Work – Using NLP in a business context (British). Knight.
Nicholas Brealey Publishing. 1995*

*Networking for Success: The NLP Approach to a Key Business and Social
Skill* – How to use NLP for networking (British). Harris. Oak Tree
Press. 2000.*

Influencing with Integrity – NLP in work situations; meetings, negotiating, etc. Laborde. Syntony Publications. 1983.

Consult Yourself: The NLP Guide to Being a Management Consultant
(British). Harris. Crown House Publishing. 2001.*

Presenting Magically. Shepherd and James. Crown House Publishing. 2001.

Sales

Sales: The Mind's Side – A simple, practical guide to selling. Robertson.
Metamorphous Press. 1990.

The Complete Sales Guide. Upsher. Mitac Ltd. 1966.

Therapy

Solutions – Practical NLP techniques applied to relationship issues. Cameron and Bandler. Future Pace, Inc. 1985.

Uncommon Therapy – Case studies of Milton Erickson. Haley. Norton. 1986.

RESOLVE: A New Model of Therapy. Bolstad. Crown House Publishing. 2002. (Also available: Double video set on the same topic.)

Peoplemaking – How to make relationships work. Satir. Science and Behaviour Books. 1972.

Phoenix – Therapeutic patterns of Milton Erickson. Gordon and Mayers-Anderson. Meta Publications. 1981.

Time

Time Line Therapy and the Basis of Personality – Bringing about change through exploration of time. James and Woodsmall. Meta Publications. 1988.

Time Lining – Developments in work with time. Bodenhamer and Hall. Anglo-American Book Co. 1997.

Modelling

Tools for Dreamers – Creativity and problem solving. Dilts et al. Meta Publication. 1991.

Strategies of Genius: Modelling Excellence (series of books). Dilts. Meta Publications. 1994 onwards.

The Emprint Method: Modelling Techniques. Cameron-Bandler, Gordon and Lebeau. Real People Press. 1985.

Know How – Personal development workbook. Cameron-Bandler, Gordon and Lebeau. Future Pace. 1985.

Associated Topics

Seven Kinds of Smart – Accelerated learning principles and practice made simple. Armstrong. Plume. 1999.*

Super Teaching: NLP and Accelerated Learning Techniques – An excellent guide for teachers and trainers. Jensen. Turning Point for Teachers. 1995.*

Creative Imagery – Visualization techniques. Fezler. Simon and Schuster. 1989.

The 20-Minute Break: Techniques for Personal Effectiveness. Rossi. Jeremy P. Tarcher, Inc. 1991*

Brain Gym for Business. Dennis, Dennis and Toplitz. Edu-Kines. 1994.

Smart Moves. Hannaford. Great Ocean Publishing. 1995.

Precursors to NLP

Psycho-cybernetics. Maltz. Wilshire Book Co. 1960.

Science and Sanity. Korzybski. Institute of General Semantics. 1933.

Steps to an Ecology of Mind. Bateson. Ballantine Books. 1972.

Plans and the Structure of Behaviour. Miller, Gallanter and Pribram.

Audiotapes

NLP: The New Technology of Achievement – NLP skills and approaches. NLP Comprehensive and Nightingale Conant. Six tapes/CDs.

Business Applications of NLP. Ewing. Two-tape set.

Success Master with NLP. Faulkner and McDonald. Six tapes/two-tape abridgment/CDs.

Creating Irresistible Influence with NLP. Faulkner. Six tapes/CDs.

Success in Mind – NLP-based personal effectiveness tapes. Titles include: *Super Self, Handling Social Situations, Super Slimming* (British).*

The New Psycho-cybernetics. Maltz and Kennedy. Six audiotapes and one video.

Videotapes

There are videotapes available of several of the well-known figures in and around NLP, including Richard Bandler, Milton Erickson and

Virginia Satir. Because the technology was not very advanced at the time they were made, the quality of some of these tapes may be poor. If you are interested in videotapes, they can be obtained from Anglo-American Books, either on sale or on loan through their Video Library.

For a complete list of NLP books, contact Anglo-American books *(see Useful Addresses)*.

Magazines and Journals

There are several NLP-based periodicals throughout the world. At time of publication, the following were known about:

UK

Rapport. The Association for Neuro-Linguistic Programming
NLP News. The International NLP Trainers' Association.

USA

Anchorpoint
The NLP Connection

Germany

MultiMind

Useful Contact Details

The Association for Neuro-Linguistic Programming (ANLP)
PO Box 5, Haverfordwest, SA63 4YA
Tel: 0870 787 1978
Email: caroline.anlp@dial.pipex.com
The Association provides information on NLP, produces a magazine and runs conferences.

NeuroLinguistic Psychotherapy and Counselling Association (NLPtCA)
Tel. 01254 826293
Email: administration@nlptca.com
Provides information on, and a route to accreditation in, NeuroLinguistic psychotherapy.

The International Neuro-Linguistic Programming Trainers' Association
Tel: 013 2928 5353
Email: inlpta@btclick.com
INLPTA is a worldwide association which independently measures the results of its members' NLP training.

The Anglo-American Book Company Ltd
Crown Buildings, Bancyfelin, Carmarthen, SA33 5ND, Wales, UK
Tel: 01267 211880
Email: books@anglo-american.co.uk
Anglo-American runs a mail-order service worldwide, for NLP books, tapes and CDs, and produces a newsletter and a range of booklists on NLP and other topics.

NLP Comprehensive

PO Box 927, Evergreen, CO 80437, USA
Tel: 1 800 233 1657, 1 303 987 2224
Website: www.nlpco.com
Suppliers of NLP books, tapes and CDs.

Management Magic (Carol Harris)

PO Box 47, Welshpool, Powys, SY21 7NX, Wales, UK
Tel: 01938 553430
Email: management.magic@effectiveconsulting.org.uk
Management Magic specializes in the development of people and organizations. It runs in-house and open NLP-based courses in personal and business skills and carries out consultancy, coaching, mentoring and facilitation as well as publishing books and audiotapes. Its sister company, Pentre Publications, produces *Effective Consulting* magazine.

Index